90 Years of Winemaking

By

Richard Schumm

ISBN: 0-7596-8766-8

This book is printed on acid free paper.

1stBooks - rev. 06/06/02

DEDICATION

To my wife Eunice

My grandparents, Joseph and Angelina De Franco,

And in memory of my dear friend, George F. Talarico

Special thanks to
Missi Boyer
Schuylkill Haven, PA
For designing many of my wine labels
One adopted for this cover.

Contact the Author at: richschumm@aol.com

Visit his website at: www.homemadewine.info

TABLE OF CONTENTS

American Wine History..1
Early Experiences In Wine Making 3
Uncle Pete And Aunt Loretta De Pasque Taralle.........................6
Pepper-Walnut Biscotti 7
Rich's Spicy Taralles..10
What Type Of Wine To Make?...12
Basic Equipment..13
Basic Wine Chemicals..18
Buying Grapes..19
Choosing You Grapes 20
Testing The Grapes 22
Brix / Specific Gravity / Potential Alcohol 23
Sanitation...26
Basic Wine Information 28
Grape Yields...28
Must..29
Fermentation Heat 30
Color Extraction 32
Making Your Wine...33
Crushing The Grapes..35
Adding Sulfites...38
Types Of Yeast...41
Pressing 46
Racking...49
Bottling...53
Corking The Bottles 56
Wine Ageing 57
White Wines..60
Steps For Making White And Blush Wines 63
Adjust Ment..65
Advanced Equipment 67
Advanced Variations 71
Blending 73
Home Made Wine Blends 76
Clarifying Additives...82
Malo-Lactic Fermentation 85
Record Keeping..90
Port Wine..93
Aquadde Wine, Piquette, Sugar Or Second Wine......................96

Fruit Wines...99
Vin Santo, Italian Dessert Wine...101
Ice Wine Or Eiswein (Dessert Wine)....................................103
Winemaking Mistakes...107
Serving Wine..113
Liqueurs..115
Advanced Winemaking Chemicals 120
Wine Grape Varities..123
European Wines 130
Charts And Conversions...133
Wine Making Suppliers...137

AMERICAN WINE HISTORY

Wine making and wine consumption has a long history in the United States. Starting in about 1619, European settlers in Virginia and along the Eastern Seaboard tried unsuccessfully to produce grapes and wine.

Although, unknown to eastern settlers, Spanish settlers in Texas and New Mexico were growing grapes and producing wine beginning about 1626. It was about 1779 that the Franciscan Monks began producing grapes and then wine in California, as we know it now.

According to a story found in the diary relating a story told by General Hamilton referring to President George Washington. General Hamilton in discussing the President "that General Washington notwithstanding his perfect regularity and love of decorum could bear to drink more wine than most people. He loved to make a procrastinated dinner- made it a rule to drink a glass of with everyone at the table and yet always drink 3-4 or more glasses of wine after dinner, according to his company".

Thomas Jefferson, our third President and wine expert was unable to produce wine from his estate in Monticello, although having tried for almost 50 years. Thomas Jefferson wrote, "Good wine is a daily necessity for me". To encourage America to drink wine, President Jefferson kept taxes low on wine and stated, "no nation is drunken where wine is cheap, hence wine should be the nations drink". Jefferson called wine a "necessary of life. He made notes on German and Italian grape growing and planted vineyards at Monticello. Jefferson predicted that America some day would make wines as good as those of France.

It was not until about 1806 in Indiana that the first commercial wines were produced in the United States. Ohio then followed suit.

Lets jump to 1919, it was the start of prohibition that home winemaking really took off. Because of a Constitutional amendment, alcohol was prohibited from being made, sold or distributed. It was because of a loophole in the law that allowed private citizens to make up to 200 gallons of wine per year. In 1933, the 18th amendment was repealed. During this period of alcohol prohibition, many of the homemade wines were terrible. People wanted alcoholic beverages and we all know the stories about the rum running gangsters. Today, we can still produce 200 gallons of wine a year for home consumption under federal law. Some states, such as New Jersey require a state home winemaking permit. Contact your state alcoholic regulatory agency. Even today, we tax payers are prohibited from distilling our own alcohol. Some countries, such as New Zealand allow individuals to distill their own alcohol for their own consumption. Just as we have amateur wine competitions, they also have competitions for home-distilled liquors.

No history of wine can be complete without mentioning the bible. The first miracle by Jesus was during the marriage celebration at Cana, where Jesus turned water into wine. The thought of being denied wine is indeed a punishment. Wine was so important that as punishment, Israel was denied wine. Enough of this very brief history lets make wine.

EARLY EXPERIENCES IN WINE MAKING

SALUTE

My indoctrination into amateur winemaking began at an early age. As a young boy of 8 or 9 years old, one of my biggest thrills was to assist during wine season. My grandfather, Joseph De Franco, was the wine maker. My uncles would all get together to help my grandfather make wine. It was truly an experience shared by the entire family. All of my cousins and myself still have find memories of tasting the sweet grape juice than ran freely from the press. The extended family would all help, Uncles and cousins with Grand Mom making the special snacks.

Unlike in the United States, wine in most European countries was and is considered a food. Wine is enjoyed by everyone, children and adults alike being a basic commodity and served at most every meal.

The wine process began in the late summer with washing, cleaning and preparing the wine barrels. Wine cellar preparation began in late summer, right after tomato season. The wood barrels (used whiskey barrels) would be taken from the cellar into the yard and cleaned. In those days, a sulfur stick was burned in the barrel to sanitize the barrels. The use of burning sulfur is called *Mechage* by the French. One of the tricks used by my grandfather to help clean the barrels was to put a piece of steel chain in the barrel. This would help clean the inside as it was rocked back and forth. Although oak barrels were used, as they got older very often wax was melted and the entire inside of the barrel was coated with this wax. Since then, I've learned that this practice was very common in Italy were chestnut barrels were used to store wine. I was very fortunate to watch and learn from these experienced home winemakers. Very often, they did not know why certain steps were taken, the traditions were passed on from one generation to the next. My curiosity about wine and enjoyment was born during this time. Many years later, after reading many books on wine and winemaking, I've come to truly appreciate the old techniques used by my grandfather, great grandfather and I'm sure for generations before. I'll get into the techniques that I was originally taught.

I was fortunate enough to have my Aunt Josephine De Franco from Voluturino, Italy recently visit and watch me make wine. During every step, she related how wine is still made in the small towns and villages in Italy. The steps she described were exactly how my grandfather made wine. The wine makers in these small towns do not vary in how their wine has been made for generation after generation. In my Aunts case, the grapes used (names unknown) have been grown on the same lands for possible hundreds of years. My 2 Aunts still today make their own wine from grapes they grow.

After time was spent preparing the barrels, cleaning the press, cleaning the cantina, which is Italian for wine cellar, it was time to visit the railroad yards in Newark, NJ. At that time, California wine grapes were brought in by rail in refrigerated rail cars. The grapes were usually bought sometime around Columbus Day. My grandfather's cantina, wine cellar, was specifically built as a wine cellar when he built his home. This wine room was all masonry including the poured concrete ceiling, keeping his wine at a constant temperature all year round. Along the one side of the room were barrel racks for holding the 4 large barrels that were filled every year. On the other side of the room were 2 shelves built to hold 10 **carboys** on each. A carboy is a 5-gallon glass container. In addition, several **demi-johns** lined the shelves. A demi-john is a glass container from 10-12 gallons. Finally on the third side was the wine press bolted to the floor that I still use today. Although my grand father passed away over 20 years ago, I still use this wine room today to make our wine. My grandmother still resides there and at 94 still enjoys the winemaking. Imagine this little old lady at 94, coming down the cellar to the wine room with a glass in hand, ready to sample whatever wine we are working with, then to go back upstairs to watch television while sipping the wine. Occasionally, she comes back down, glass still in her hand, saying this wine was very good, looking for another glass.

It was usually Sunday morning, time to buy grapes with Grandpop. I was excited, and still to this day, going to buy grapes is an exciting time to me, bringing back many fond memories of my childhood. Sunday morning would arrive, I would get in the dump truck with Grandpop along with my Uncle Anthony De Franco. Once at the rail yards, there was a hustle and bustle as in any terminal market, yet all the people here were looking for wine grapes. Venders displaying the grapes, yelling prices, buyers looking and tasting.

Most of the grape buyers at that time were immigrants that brought their customs and love of wine making to America. For a youngster, I was amazed listening to all the buyers and sellers supposed speaking English, yet I could hardly understand any of them. All the Mediterranean countries were represented. As with all these immigrants, winemaking was a pleasure and a source of pride. Each made the best wine. As we walked from rail car to railcar, each lot of grape was sampled by eating a few. With each taste came a discussion of price and quality.

The number one rule in winemaking. Get the best quality grapes you can. No matter how good a winemaker might be, you cannot turn inferior grapes into great wine.

Once a grape was decided upon, we would revisit that rail car, again, climbing in, to re-taste the grapes. Now the price haggling started, back and forth between buyer and seller. This haggling went on until a price was agreed upon for a certain, particular grape. This meant very specific boxes of grape. Grapes, as they still do, came packed in wood boxes from 36 to 42 pounds each depending on variety.

At this time, someone would go for the truck, and the other person would watch the grape that was to be purchased. As I was told, you had to watch the grape, otherwise the venders would switch lots, giving you a lesser quality grape. Grapes should be clean, no mold, free from juice running out of the box. This diligent watch would continue up until the grape boxes were actually loaded on the truck. As you can see, trust was somewhat limited in the rail yards of Newark, NJ.

Also at the rail yard, new and used whiskey barrels were sold, along with a few other winemaking supplies. Getting wine chemicals, although, few if any were ever used, was a major problem, having to go to New York to buy them.

On the way home, fresh bread was always bought from the old brick oven bakeries that existed in Newark. Once arriving home with the grapes, grandmom could come out as we unloaded the truck to taste the various grapes that were just bought. A few bowls of wine grape were always saved to be eaten fresh later in the day, after the grape was crushed. The crushing is known as *Pigiatura* in Italian.

Once the truck was unloaded, my Uncle Lou De Franco and my cousin's would arrive to help with the crushing. For an hour or so, we would search around for bolts in order to attach the motor to the grape crusher. This was a hand-operated crusher that my grand father converted to a motorized crusher. This motor served a dual purpose as I grinder for sharpening knives and chisels. The motor had a pulley attached by way of a fan belt connected to a pulley on the crusher. At the time in the mid 1960's, this crusher was at least 50 years old. We used this crushr until just a few years ago, when we bought a new crusher-destemer. The old crusher would shake, rattle, make lots of noise, and you had to be carefully of the fan belt flying off the pulleys. The opened boxes of grape were crushed into wood barrels with the one side of the barrel removed. The 2 flat sides of a barrel are called the heads.

My job was to remove the wood tops from the wine boxes, and after the boxes were empty, to carefully take the boxes apart. At that time, the 2 sides of these grape boxes were pine; to be used later by my cousin Joe, my brother Joe and myself to make little wood projects, as boys will do. The remainder of the boxes were stacked to be used in the potbelly stove in my grandfathers work shed behind the garage. Grape boxes were never put out in front of the house as garbage. One reason was we used the wood to make little projects, but more importantly, my Grand father came to America to become an American. Not that he denied his heritage or culture, but he believed that neighbors would think that he was un-American or too ethnic by putting out grape boxes. Immigrant's years ago, became Americans, wanted to be American and were very proud that they were Americans. It's a mindset that's difficult to explain. He was of the generation whose sons went to war in Europe. The sons of immigrants that fought and died for their new homeland. Years ago, there was much bias towards all ethnic groups, every nationality of immigrant was looked upon with suspicion or more. The old timers worked very hard at learning English and the American way. I better get off the soapbox and continue.

After the crushing took place, everything cleaned, boxes broken up and put away. The open ended wood barrels were covered with wood for nature to do its work. No yeast was added. Because the crusher only crushed the grapes, the stems were included in the barrels. Nowadays the stems are usually removed. Once the barrels were covered we would all go into cellar den area. This finished basement room with bar was used for many family parties including the traditional Christmas Eve with the 7 fish dinner that lasted till midnight.

During the earliest wine making days with Grand pop, we were all there. Sitting at the tables, wine would be poured. My Grandfather would lift his glass to everyone and say "Salute". Grandmom would bring out a plate of sharp Provolone along with fresh bread we bought earlier. Platters of all our traditional foods would be served along with tarralles. Hard Tarrales, extremely good with wine, are an Italian type of Pretzel, no salt, round and very hard. The tarrarels would be flavored with black pepper or fennel flavored. (Recipe below)

Uncle Pete and Aunt Loretta De Pasque Taralle

6 cups of flour
¾ cup of olive oil
¾ cup water
3 large eggs
1-teaspoon salt
3 tablespoon of black pepper
2 packages of dry yeast
½ cup of sugar
Fennel seeds if desired (1-3 tablespoon)

Combine all the ingredients, knead well
Let sit, covered with plastic for ½ hour

Roll out the dough to about ½ inch thick. With a knife, cut strips about ½ inch thick, you will then have rows or strips about ½ inch by ½ inch. These are the rolled slightly so the long strips are rounded, like fat pasta.

These are then cut to about 4-6 inches long and both ends connected so that they are round similar to a bagel.

In a large pot of boiling water, place the formed rings. When the tarrales float, remove them from the boiling water with a slotted spoon. Allow to dry. This are placed on a cookie sheet and baked at 425 degrees until well cooked.

Taralle di Vino (Red Wine Biscuits)

4 cups Flour
3/4-cup sugar
2-teaspoon salt
1-tablespoon double acting baking powder
1-cup full body HOME MADE red wine
1-cup olive oil

Combine 4 cups of flour, sugar, salt and baking powder, mix well. Mix the oil and red wine slowly into the flour mixture. The dough will be soft, add additional flour if the mixture is still sticky. Cut dough into 40 equal pieces, rolling each piece into 4-5 inch long "rope". Form the "rope" into circles similar to a bagel. In a large pot of boiling water, place the formed rings. When the tarrales float, remove them from the boiling water with a slotted spoon. Allow to dry. Then bake the rings at 350 degrees for 20 minutes. Reduce the heat to 300 degrees and bake for an additional 15 minutes until golden brown. Cool and store in airtight containers. Great to nibble while sipping your homemade wine.

Pepper-Walnut Biscotti

1 ¾ Cup Flour
½ teaspoon baking soda
½ teaspoon baking powder
1/8-teaspoon salt
½ teaspoon black pepper
1-cup sugar
½ cup butter
2 teaspoon orange peel
2 eggs large
½ teaspoon almond extract
1 ½ teaspoon vanilla extract
1-½ cups walnuts, Toasted.

Sift together flour, baking soda, powder, black pepper and salt. Cream the softened butter lightly with electric mixer, add the sugar slowly and mix till fluffy. Mix together flour mixture and butter blend. Cover dough and refrigerate until chilled (1 hour in frig). Pre-heat oven to 350 degrees. Divide dough into 3

7

equal pieces. Roll the pieces into 1-½ inch diameter logs. Place 1 log onto buttered cookie sheets. Bake 20 minutes till brown. Cut logs diagonally in ¾ inch strips. Again, place each strip back onto cookie sheet, on side. Bake an additional 15 minutes till golden brown. Cool and store in airtight containers.

Fresh Mozzarella with Roasted Red Sweet Peppers

Fresh Mozzarella (not the kind in plastic wrap sold in supermarkets), but fresh, stored in water at Italian stores. This was sliced and put on a platter, served along with grand moms, home roasted red sweet peppers that are marinated for a few hours with olive oil and garlic. The roasted red sweet peppers were laid along side the fresh mozzarella and the olive oil marinade drizzled on top of the mozzarella. Served with fresh, crunchy Italian bread.

Cured Meat Platter

We always had a platter of dried sausage/salami. This platter would include dried soppresata (usually home made), (similar to a salami), prosutto, dried sweet and hot sausage (again home made, it is sausage that has been dry cured), and Genoa salami. All of which is sliced paper-thin.

EARLY EXPERIENCES

During the week after crushing or *Pigiatura*, every morning before work and a second time after work, Grandpop or I would go to the wine cellar and press down the cap of floating skins and stems in the barrel.

Everyday, we would press down the cap of crushed skins and stems that would rise to the top of the barrel during fermentation. We would check to see if the wine was "boiling" or "*bollitura*" yet. The word bollitura means boiling in Italian and the old timers referred to fermentation as boiling. Although the old timers did not directly care about fermentation temperature, I was always told that if the wine did not start to boil in 3 days, we had to keep the door to the wine room open. This would allow some heat into the wine room and allow the boiling or fermentation to begin.

After exactly one week, the following Sunday, it would be time to press the grape that have been fermenting. First, the bottom bung of the upright barrel was removed, and the free-run juice was taken out of the fermenting barrel and put into the wood barrel. The fermentation barrel was always raised off the floor so that air could circulate under the barrel and not touch the cold floor. This fermentation barrel would have a hole in the bottom, about 1-inch with a bung in place. This bung was knocked out and the free run juice would run out. We always had a half-barrel under the fermenting barrel to catch the juice. This ½ barrel would have the farthest side about 12 inches taller so the juice would be caught. After removing the free-run juice, the crushed grape were removed and put into the press. The grape press or wine press was known as the *Torchio* in Italian. Since only naturally occurring yeast (found on the grape skins themselves) was used for fermentation, the juice at this point was very sweet. All the grand children would take turns with a little shot glass with a handle, sipping the juice as it flowed from the old press. NO commercial yeast was ever used. Most wild yeast's cannot be guaranteed to fully ferment the sugars in grape. The old timers relied solely on the natural occurring yeast's which in many cases, did cause problems later on, such as stuck fermentation, off odors, sweet wines, etc.

After pressing. The pressed skin and stems is called *"Vinnacce"* in Italian. If the grape must or Vinnacce was not pressed too hard, a second wine was occasionally made. This second wine was called *Aquadde*. I have detailed instructions later in the book.

Usually, the Vinnacce was used in the garden as compost. It is this same Vinnacce that is the basis for *Grappa*, a strong, harsh Italian brandy. This Grappa is also called *Marc* (french) or *Tresterbrannt* XE "Tresterbrannt", in German. Although it is illegal to distill any alcohol in the Unites States, I've heard of many old timers that would make Grappa from the Vinnacce.

The juice from the press was added to the free-run juice into the barrels and there this barrel would continue to ferment, foaming across the top of the barrel, sometimes the wine was sweet, sometimes it wasn't. Some years, the wine was a bit *FRISSANTE*, which is carbon dioxide. Carbon Dioxide is a naturally occurring by-product of fermentation. I am not referring to intentional bubbles in the wine, which is champagne or sparkling wine. A wine that is Frissante or Fizzy is a wine that all the sugar was not fully fermented when bottled. This is the same Carbon Dioxide found in Champagne or Sparkling wine but in lesser amounts. Champagne or proper terminology Sparkling wine bottles and corks are specifically designed to contain the higher pressures of carbon dioxide and will not burst as will happen to regular wine bottles.

Very often, these old timers wine would be a little sweet that would start to ferment again in the spring. Many of these old timers blamed this on certain variety grapes or that the wine woke up in the spring. The quality of the wine from these amateurs varied greatly from superb to barely drinkable. Some of the old timers made a blend of red and white grapes, making a dark rose that was usually very strong.

In the early spring, usually the week before Good Friday, the wine was racked for the final time. The final racking in Italian is the *'Travasare*. One barrel's worth was put into 5-gallon glass containers called carboys or larger glass containers called Demi-Johns. A barrel was never left started without being fully emptied. No one could tell me why, but had to be done. From the 5-gallon carboys, individual bottles were filled daily as needed. Many old timers took wine daily direct from the wood barrels. To help prevent the wine from oxidation, olive oil was poured in the barrel to form a light film covering the wine. This practice is now very rare and I guess it did prevent the air from coming in contact with the wine, but it surely didn't do much for the barrel.

As I got older, in my early teens, we ate over my grand parents at least twice per week. It was my job to go to the cantina to fill the bottle for dinner Grandpop always told me to whistle as I went to get the wine. His reasoning was that if I was whistling I would not be drinking the wine. To this day, I still can't whistle.

To this day, I credit my grandfather, Joseph De Franco, for my love of winemaking, the fond memories, since our wine making was a family gathering He was born in 1899 in Volturino, Italy having been taught how to make wine by his father, Luigi De Franco. To this day, we have relatives that still make wine from grapes grown on the property at the same house in Volturino, Italy.

I continued to help my grandfather make wine until my late teens when he passed away. After a few years, while I was in my mid to late twenties. I decided I wanted to make wine. I spoke to my Uncle, who was still making wine the way my grandfather did, listened to his explanation and I went about making my wine, the old way. The first year, a friend of mine wanted to help, and did. He went to the grape markets, looking for grape I did as a child. Problem was, I had no idea what type of grape we used. I knew what my grand father called them, I asked for pera si grape, and no one had any inclination what I was talking about till I found this old timer, who recognized the broken English version of Petit Sirah. **I believe the key to making good wine is simply paying attention to details.**

Rich's Spicy Taralles

3 cups self-rising flour
1-tablespoon black pepper
1-tablespoon fennel seeds
1-tablespoon hot pepper
1-teaspoon garlic powder
1-cup warm water
½ cup oil oil

Combine all the ingredients, knead well
Let sit, covered with plastic for ½ hour

Roll out the dough to about ½ inch thick. With a knife, cut strips about ½ inch thick, you will then have rows or strips about ½ inch by ½ inch. These are the rolled slightly so the long strips are rounded, like fat pasta.

These are then cut to about 4-6 inches long and both ends connected so that they are round similar to a bagel.

In a large pot of boiling water, place the formed rings. When the tarrales float, remove them from the boiling water with a slotted spoon. Allow to dry.

This are placed on a cookie sheet and baked at 425 degrees until well cooked.

WHAT TYPE OF WINE TO MAKE?

Let me start by saying anyone can make wine. My 70-year-old Aunts in Italy still make their own wine and so can you. Whether you live in an apartment and want to make a few gallons or have access to a nice basement or garage, anyone can make wine.

One of the first questions you have to ask yourself, is what type of wine do you want to make. Every year, we make 5-6 different types of wines, always experimenting with one or two new blends or varieties. Included is our old stand-by blend, which is always the largest batch. This blend has taken years for me to develop but suits my taste and that's your basic guide, make what you like. Over time, you will notice how some wines improve with age and others do not, but are great drinking new. In some cases, we just can't keep the wine long enough to tell how it will age in time, particularly the new experiments that turn out great and are easy drinking. Sometimes, the experiments will turn out bitter disappointments, such as a huge batch of raspberry wine we made. After many attempts to correct the wine and age it, improvement never occurred. With each new batch of wine, you will hone your winemaking skills. Learn from your mistakes and keep accurate records of what you did and when. I'll get into record keeping later. Don't get disgusted if you have a batch that isn't quite right, we all, including professional wine makers occasionally get those batches, not quite right. My book will help you make good quality wine.

How do you decide what wine to make? I started making my own wine several years after my grandfather passed away, using all his old equipment and barrels. I used the same variety grapes that he did. What a disaster. Everyone told me the wine was good and OK, but no body wanted gallons of it. Your taking the correct first step, read a book on winemaking, I never did at first. Since then, I've read many books on winemaking, taken courses and now have over 20 years of winemaking experience, plus the knowledge from my grandfather that I can now understand. Most old timers made one type of wine, usually a red. The few that made "white" wine you would not recognize as a white, as it was usually dark in color, from amber to light brown. It tasted very nice but is not accepted by today's standards of white wine.

From many years of experience, I would recommend that a beginner make a red wine. I have always found it much harder to make a high quality white wine than a red. The white wines are much more delicate and must be pampered a bit. Start with a red wine.

Try the varietal (single type of grape) wines, keep a log of the wines you try, what you like about them. You will learn for example that Merlot is a soft red wine or Alicante provides great rich color (great for blending). Many of the commercial wineries state on the label what type of grapes are used and the percentage of each variety. By federal law, as an example, a commercial wine labeled as Zinfandel must contain at least 70% zinfandel grape to be called zinfandel, but no additional varieties are required to be listed. This is a Federal-labeling requirement for commercial wineries. Buy a range of different variety wines, taste them, take notes, and try blending a few and I'll discuss blending later.

This book is primarily about wine from grape although, I've made and also tasted very good wines made from every fruit you can imagine. Lets focus on wines from grapes. Today, the home winemaker has a large selection of wine grapes and juices available. Remember our goal is to satisfy our taste buds by making high quality wines at home. Experiment; try different grapes and different blends of grapes. Most commercial wineries are making wines for mass-market appeal. It's not until you try the premium, expensive wines that you will be able to compare, good homemade wines. In a short time, you will fine tune your methods, and produce premium wine at home.

Your biggest critic will be yourself, make wines that you, your family and friends will enjoy. Just as wine making was a family social gathering when I grew up, so is drinking the home made wine. Start by making a wine variety you like, start with a basic varietal, weather you buy fresh wine grapes in the fall or any of the many wine grape juices available all year round from the many home winemaking supply stores.

One of the joys of home winemaking is bringing a few bottles or a jug of great homemade wine, when you go visiting. Growing up, before my Grandfather went to a party, a gallon jug of his best wine was filled, to be brought along. Friends and relatives always enjoyed this. Well made homemade wines very often have much more body and flavor than commercial wines, and many people truly appreciate fine quality home made wines.

SALUTE and enjoy your own homemade wine.

BASIC EQUIPMENT

There is actually very little needed to convert grapes into some sort of wine product, nature can do it all, but there will be so many variables that could render the wine undrinkable. Put the grapes into a container and sha-zam, a few weeks later wine. I'm not telling you to do this, but grapes will turn into wine with very little help from man. Grapes are the only fruit that contain enough sugar and acids, naturally blended together to make a wine that will not spoil and of course, treated properly.

HYDROMETER

The first piece of equipment that you should obtain is called a *HYDROMETER also known as Saccharometer* and belongs in every wine cellar. A triple scale 0- 30 brix wine hydrometer is glass tube similar to a thermometer and is available at your local or mail order wine making supply shop. A wine hydrometer is fairly inexpensive, under $20.00. This instrument is used to measure the amount of sugar in your wine juice. This grape juice is called must. The term for the amount of sugar in your wine is called **BRIX**. Without a hydrometer, you could never determine the amount of sugar in your grape/juice. The hydrometer also gives you an idea of the amount of alcohol that will be produced from the available sugar in your wine juice or properly referred to as must. Be aware that, you will not be accurately determining the alcohol content of your wine. For a rough estimate, for every 2 degrees of sugar or brix, fermentation will yield about 1 percent alcohol. This is only a rough estimate. The French wine hydrometer is called a saccharometer and measures potential alcohol on the Dujardin scale. In Germany, the hydrometer measures on the Oechsle scale. All these scales are basically measuring the specific gravity or solids in the liquid. Just a note, a hydrometer should read 1.000 in plain water.

Do not put your hydrometer directly into your juice. This instrument is made of glass and is easily broken. You do not want to contaminate your wine with slivers of glass, so be careful.

The proper way to use a hydrometer is to obtain some juice in a graduated cylinder or clean glass jar. If you are obtaining the grape juice from crushed grapes, pour the juice through a piece of cheesecloth to roughly filter out the skins and particles. Fill the glass jar with juice and slowly place the hydrometer into the juice. Do not drop it in, you can break it. The hydrometer will settle into the juice and you will read the Brix or specific gravity reading at the point the hydrometer settles into the wine at the point the wine meets the floating hydrometer. This point is called the meniscus level.

Be sure to clean your hydrometer after each use and store in a safe place were it would not be broken.

PRIMARY FERMENTATION CONTAINER

The next piece of equipment is a container to initially ferment your grape juice. Forget about grandmoms old clay crock. Do not use aluminum containers. The primary fermentation container can be made out of glass, such as a carboy, or food grade plastic pails and drums, or stainless steel pails and drums. The amount of wine that you planning to make in this batch will determine the size of the primary fermentation container. If you are buying 6 gallons of juice, your primary fermentation container should have a capacity of 7 ½ gallons. The primary fermentation container should be 25-30% larger than the volume you're putting in. If you are buying fresh grapes, again, the same rule stands. This additional room is for all for foaming during fermentation.

If you're buying juice, a glass carboy can be used for your primary fermentation container. For our batches, we use food grade plastic 55gallon drums with the one end cut out. We usually put about 400—500 pounds of crushed grapes in these drums for primary fermentation. Smaller drums can be used for smaller amounts. Plastic garbage cans are not really a good choice, they are not usually food grade plastic, and more importantly, most have lots of crevices and indentations for wild bacteria to hide. I must admit though, that on occasion, if I am short on primary fermentation containers, I will use a new plastic garbage can. We used to use wood barrels for primary fermentation but I don't recommend using them. They are more trouble than they are worth, between leaks and being difficult to clean and are very heavy. Remember; never use any metal besides stainless steel while wine making.

MEASURING SPOONS

Another item that's needed are measuring spoons like those used in the kitchen. Your better off getting your own complete set for wine making so the wife won't come hunting looking for them. I like the spoons all attached on a ring with several sizes from ¼ teaspoon to 1 tablespoon. Individual spoons measure any additives you might be adding to the wine more accurately. Another plus is that if all the spoons are on a ring, you won't loose any. I keep all my small wine equipment, testing kits and chemicals in plastic toolboxes. All the equipment is neat and more importantly, easily found.

FERMENTATION LOCKS or AIR LOCKS

Fermentation Locks also known air locks are needed whether you are making 1 gallon of homemade dandelion wine or 100 gallons of cabernet. Fermentation locks are very inexpensive and are made from either plastic or glass. The purpose of an airlock is to allow the carbon dioxide that is created during fermentation to escape but prohibit any air (along with wild yeast and bacteria) from entering the fermentation container. Air locks are not used during preliminary fermentation but during secondary fermentation. There are several types of air locks, but all perform the same function, allow the carbon dioxide to escape while stopping air from entering. If fermentation locks were not used, either the container will explode from the pressure, or at the very least, the cork will be blown out, allowing air, bacteria and fruit flies to enter, which could all cause your wine to go bad. I find the plastic one-piece fermentation lock the best, I've always lost parts to the multi part lock but that's your choice.

15

Along with the plastic fermentation or air locks, you will buy rubber stoppers with a hole pre drilled for the air lock, these are called bored rubber stoppers. Rubber stoppers come in various sizes suitable for gallon jugs to wood barrels. Be sure the stopper fits the container for secondary fermentation. Its good to have several sizes on hand, just in case you need additional containers for secondary fermentation. Again, store all your unused equipment clean.

FUNNELS

It seems I'm always buying funnels, a different size funnel for every job. At the minimum, you will need one funnel, preferable plastic. Do not use aluminum. You will use the funnel to pour your juice once it has completed primary fermentation into your secondary fermentation container. Be sure the funnel fits the secondary fermentation container properly. There are several types of winemaking funnels. One funnel has a built in strainer, to remove any grape berries and seeds that might be floating in your juice. Another funnel made just to fill bottles, has a small handle on top that allows you to lift the partially filled funnel to the next bottle without spilling the contents of the funnel. This same funnel automatically stops when the bottle is filled. Again, these funnels are inexpensive and made of plastic.

CLEAR PLASTIC SIPHON HOSE

You will need about 5 feet of clear plastic or flexible PVC tubing, ½ inch diameter for racking your wine from one container to another. For smaller batches of fewer than 5 gallons, ¼ inch diameter tubing may be used. This tubing is available at better hardware stores or wine supply shops. Do not use old garden hose, use new plastic tubing and keep it clean. I prefer clear food grade polyvinyl tubing so I can watch the juice being transferred. For as many years as I remember my grandfather making wine, he used a black rubber hose for transferring the wine. In those days, there was no clear tubing available to home winemakers. Not that I minded, but every time I assisted in siphoning or racking the wine, I wound up with a mouthful of wine.

SECONDARY FERMENTATION CONTAINER

The most common secondary fermentation container for the home winemaker is a 5-gallon glass container called a carboy. These too are available from winemaking supply shops. You can get carboys in several sizes but the 5-gallon carboy is the most common. Along with the secondary fermentation container you will need a rubber stopper that fits properly (hole in center) and a fermentation or air lock. Clean 1 gallon Glass jugs can also be used but be sure the bored rubber stopper fits properly.

BASIC WINE CHEMICALS

SULFUR DIOXIDE

Sulfur dioxide has been used in wine since the Middle Ages. Sulfur dioxide inhibits bacterial growth and mold growth in wine. It is the single most important chemical used in virtually all wine making. Sulfur dioxide is not a cure all for mis-handled wine, but will help your wine stay healthy and retain its color.

Sulfur dioxide is the only chemical that you will need as a beginner. As a rule with all chemicals in winemaking, use as little as possible. A good wine only needs sulfur dioxide.

Sulfur dioxide is available in several forms for the home winemaker. The most commonly used for smaller batches of wine are **CAMPDEN TABLETS**. These tablets (similar in size to an aspirin) are simple and easy to use for the beginner. Each tablet will provide about 75 parts per million (PPM) of sulfur dioxide per gallon on juice/wine. The usual rate to be used is about ½ tablet per gallon. These tablets must be crushed prior to adding to your juice or wine.

The form of sulfur dioxide I prefer is called **Potassium Metabisulfite** and is in powder form. You would use ¼ teaspoon of Potassium Metabisulfite per 5 gallons of juice/wine that would give you about 40-45 PPM of sulfur dioxide (So2).

Both these chemicals are readily available through suppliers of winemaking equipment.

I don't want to get too technical at this point, but as your techniques improve and become more advanced, there are variations of sulfur addition do to variations of pH.

Before we start making our wine, let's discuss the various types of wines

BUYING GRAPES

Great wines come from GREAT Grapes. An important consideration for all winemakers to remember is that fine wine begins on the vine. If you're lucky enough to live in an area with local wine grapes, try the local grapes

For most of us home winemakers; our grapes must be shipped from California. Our other choice is to find local American/ French Hybrid grapes. California grows 90% of the wine grapes grown in the United States. The wine grapes grown in California are Vinifera as those in Europe. If you want to try winemaking without buying fresh grapes, most winemaking supply houses offer wine grape juice either fresh or frozen in plastic pails.

My winemaking friends and I, usually buy some local New Jersey grown hybrid grapes. It's an adventure and fun time to go to a vineyard, and watch the grapes you are buying getting picked. Some farmers will let you pick your own grapes for a small savings in cost.

Start you hunt for wine grapes early. Start asking other winemakers in your area where you can purchase fresh wine grapes. Another source of information will be your wine or brew supply shop. The owners are usually knowledgeable. Usually in late August or early September, the fresh fruit and vegetable wholesale or terminal markets will begin carrying wine grapes, but start your search early.

Early August is a good time to start your hunt. In many areas, the wine grape merchants are seasonal and are only open during the grape season. Go visit the merchant once you are able to find fresh grapes. Talk to him. Ask him when the grapes should arrive. Ask him what varieties will be offering for sale. Find out if he refrigerates the grapes upon arrival.

The wine grape business is changing. Some of the distributors will crush and press fresh grapes on site for a small fee. You will choose the grapes you like and on the spot, they will crush and squeeze the grapes and fill your containers. You will bring carboys or pails with lids to carry your freshly pressed juices home. Be sure your containers are clean and sanitized. If you bring carboys, be extremely careful since they are glass. In many cases, having the fresh grapes crushed by the merchant is the most economical way to get started while still using fresh grapes.

Many of these distributors also carry pails of pressed juices that can be stored for long periods of time under refrigeration. In addition, aseptically packed boxed of juice are available.

Most times your grape distributor will be your best help. Don't be afraid to ask their advice. Many suppliers of grapes, juice and wine supplies are extremely knowledgeable in winemaking and the proper use of the many chemicals available. I've only dealt several suppliers but 2 suppliers really stick in my mind, both are fantastic. Jimmy Corrado, Joann and the entire family at Corrados Winemaking Center in Clifton, NJ www.corradosmarket.com along with Moorhead's and Boettcher's at Presque Isle Wine Cellars in North East, PA www.piwine.com. Both companies have been around a very long time and are very happy to help you, as most suppliers will.

Choosing you grapes

Since you already spoke with the distributor about what varieties will be available and have already decided what grapes you will be buying. Very often, grapes arrive early or late because of trucking problems, weather and a multitude of other problems. Be sure to have a second or third choice of what type of wine you wish to make, for whatever reason the grapes are unavailable.

We have gone to buy a certain grape, only to find out that they did not arrive yet, or another variety was shipped instead. Occasionally, I don't like the condition of the grapes that had arrived. Beware of moldy or grapes that are leaking juice.

To get the best grapes and this is a problem for those of us, not fortunate enough to live in the grape regions of California. I like to buy my grapes within a day of arrival at the distributor. This can involve several visits to the distributor. Based on my experience of being a food inspector/investigator for 20 years, several points must be looked at. To begin, most wine grapes are packed in wood boxes holding from 36 to 42 pounds of grape. First look at the boxes of grapes, are they wet and leaking juice? If so, look at other grapes. This can be from heat, over ripeness etc. Are the grapes cold and under refrigeration? Cold refrigeration slows down the effects of time on the grapes and mold growth. I prefer buying grapes that are refrigerated. All grapes are shipped in refrigerated trucks, so if your distributor does not have refrigeration, it is important to get the grapes as soon as possible after they arrive. Do you notice mold growing? Grapes cannot be washed and why bother-using grapes covered with molds that will ruin your wine.

> ➢ Buy the best quality grapes you can find. You can never make great wine with bad quality grapes.

Next, my favorite, taste the different grapes, judging for yourself the different varieties, tastes, sweetness. All the grape distributors I've ever gone to, expect you to taste the grape. Just a berry or two from each variety, its not a buffet. Look at the label for the variety. Usually the boxes are labeled or stamped with the variety by the packer. BEWARE of variety names that are hand written or unlabeled. They are unscrupulous dealers, and I've seen them, writing the names of the grapes on the boxes. I understand that one of the dealers in my area would switch boxes of grapes while loading your car or truck, switching with older, leaking grapes.

While buying grapes, you will have the opportunity to meet and talk with other winemakers in your area. Talk to them; ask questions, most people are happy to help. When you buy grapes, you are looking to buy red grapes that have about 20 to 24 degrees Brix. White wines as well as blush wines grapes would contain 19 to 23 Brix. Sparkling wine grapes would have from 18 to 20 degree Brix This is only a guideline. If the grapes contain less sugar (Brix), your wine will be low in alcohol and with that unstable and prone to spoilage. If your grapes are low in sugar, sugar can be added. Please read the chapter on sugar addition.

To learn more about the varieties of wine grapes, read the chapter of grape varieties at the end of this book.

TESTING THE GRAPES

Before you start making wine, you must test the grape for sugar content in the juice. The amount of sugar in the grape is known as degrees **BRIX** o degrees balling. As a basis, distilled water has a specific gravity of 1.000 Weather you are using fresh grapes, fresh pressed juice or refrigerated juice, you will still have to test your grapes.

A **HYDROMETER** is used to measure the BRIX of grape juice. They are available at all wine shops and are about 8 inches long, made of glass and look somewhat like a long thermometer. This is not an expensive item and can be found for a few bucks. Handle your hydrometer with care as I've broken several. You will also need a graduated cylinder to use with the hydrometer. Try to find a plastic graduated cylinder, as it won't get broken.

In order to get accurate BRIX reading from a particular LARGE lot of grapes from grape about to be harvested, I collect a 100 berry sample from throughout the bunches. Now crush each 100-berry sample; squeeze the berries through a small strainer into a jar, then pouring your liquid sample into your graduated cylinder. Carefully, slide your hydrometer into the graduated cylinder. As you look at your hydrometer, if you look closely, the liquid will be a bit higher along the hydrometer. The liquid will then curve downward slightly. Read at the bottom of the liquid curve. This is called the minicus level.

Most hydrometers will indicate Brix, specific gravity and potential alcohol Read the Brix scale and write down your results. Now, check your second sample, and again write down your results. Average the 2 results and that will be your beginning BRIX.

Now, you're wondering why should I be checking the Brix of the grape. Well, simply, to determine the potential alcohol of the finished wine. If the alcohol is too low, your wine will be unstable and flabby. If the sugar content is less than expected, sugar will be added at the time of crushing.

> ➢ Red grapes should have about 20 to 24 degrees Brix. White wines as well as blush wines grapes would contain 19 to 23 Brix. Sparkling wine grapes would have from 18 to 20 degrees Brix. This is only a guideline. I prefer my wines on the higher end on the scale. If your grape are a bit low in sugar or degrees Brix, consider adding sugar.

For smaller quantities of grapes or grape you have already purchased, you can also sample directly from your barrel of crushed grapes or liquid juice. Once your grapes are crushed and in your primary fermentation container, you can draw a sample. Use a sterilized container to dip into your fermentation container. You will have to strain this sample through a sterilized strainer, removing the skins and seeds. This strained sample can be poured into your graduated cylinder for testing with the hydrometer. After you are finished, this sample can be poured back into the fermentation container. Be aware that, you will not be accurately determining the alcohol content of your wine.

> For a rough estimate, for every 2 degrees of sugar or brix, fermentation will yield about 1 percent alcohol. This is only a rough estimate.

I continue testing every day to track the fermentation. Over the course of days, you will notice the percentage of sugar dropping and being converted to alcohol. Keep a record of your progress.

BRIX / SPECIFIC GRAVITY / POTENTIAL ALCOHOL

BRIX	SPECIFIC GRAVITY	POTENTIAL ALCOHOL
10	1.0395	5.57
11	1.0434	6.33
12	1.0475	6.90
13	1.0515	7.48
14	1.0556	8.05
15	1.0594	8.63
16	1.0639	9.20
17	1.0680	9.78
18	1.0723	10.35
19	1.0769	10.93
20	1.0814	11.50
21	1.0859	12.08
22	1.0903	12.65
23	1.0949	13.23
24	1.0994	13.80
25	1.1041	14.38

Most wine yeast usually dies off at about 14% alcohol. There are specific yeasts and methods to produce slightly higher alcohol wines.

BRIX	SPECIFIC GRAVITY	POTENTIAL ALCOHOL
26.5	1.110	15.00
27.5	1.115	16.4
28.5	1.120	16.9
29.5	1.125	17.6
30.5	1.130	18
32.0	1.135	18.9

ACID

Grapes naturally contain several types of acid. The acids found in grapes are malic, tartaric, citric, tannic and phosphoric. When we measure or test acids, amateurs do not measure each type individually, as this is very complicated and you will need a lot of test equipment. Instead we in America test for total acids. In Canada, this is referred to as testing for tartaric acid or as the French test for sulfuric acid.

Acid should be between 0.60% to 0.85%. For red wines, start with 0.65% acid and with white wines; start with 0.70% acid. Wine with less than 0.6% acid taste flat to most people and wines with over 0.9% have too much acid for enjoyable consumption. Acid test kits are available at home winemaking shops. They are inexpensive and simple to use. Follow the manufacturer's directions for acid testing.

➢ Acid test kits are called Acid Titration kits.

After you have tested your mustfor acid and found the acid level to be low, now is the time to correct the acid. You will have to add acid, available at winemaking shops.

To reduce acid, a mixture of sugar and water must be added. Enough sugar must be added so that the water is 23.5 Brix.

pH

Although pH strips known, as litmus paper (available at most wine supply stores) are not as accurate as other test methods, I believe they are accurate enough for home winemakers. With pH strips, you simply dunk your pH strip into your wine must, take the strip out and compare the color on the strip with the color chart on the container. This will give you a fairly accurate reading.

Also available are pH meters that are much more accurate and are fairly inexpensive.

Most table wines, pH, should be between 3 and 4. If the pH of the grape juice is above 3.40, tartaric acid should be added to reduce the pH to between 3.25-3.40. When the pH of must is below 3.5, the wine will ferment much more evenly.

SANITATION

The biggest problem in winemaking is lack of sanitation. After working many years for the State as a food inspector, I've learned and seen first hand the problems that lack of sanitation can cause. The same is true with wine. Just as bad eggs can turn eggnog into poison, wild bacteria and mold in your wine will sour your wine undrinkable, not even fit for vinegar.

Everything you use in winemaking must be clean, from spoons and funnels to fermentation tanks. In food processing, the USDA recommends a solution of a minimum of 100 PPM of chlorine. Since chlorine can cause pitting in stainless steel, be sure to rinse the chlorine solution off after 3 to 5 minutes contact time. Use common, unscented household bleach to make your solution.

We usually, use a spray bottle filled with our chlorine solution to spray the fermentation tanks, crusher and other large items. Smaller equipment such as fermentation locks and rubber stoppers can be washed, rinsed and sanitized in the sink. Carboys inside and out can be sanitized in the sink. Clean your equipment when you're finished and store to allow proper air circulation. It's a simple procedure; Wash, Rinse, Sanitize and Allow to air-dry.

> ➤ To make a solution of chlorine add one tablespoon of household chlorine bleach to one gallon of water. This will give you a chlorine solution of 200 PPM, which meets the U.S. Public Health Service's recommended levels for hard surface sanitation. Contact time with the chlorine solution should be a minimum of 1 minute.

Remember, wash, rinse and sanitize. After sanitizing, allow surfaces to air dry.

Instead of the chlorine solution, you can use a solution of potassium Metabisulfite, which is available at wine supply stores. To make an effective sanitizing solution, add 2 ounces of sulfite powder to 1 gallon of water. Again, rinse this solution off stainless steel, as it will cause pitting.

Clean your fermentation drums inside and out, leaving no chance for molds or stray bacteria to cause you problems. Clean and sanitize everything that will come in contact with your grape and wine.

One of the most important factors besides timing in making good wine CONSISTANTLY is proper sanitation. Keep your equipment clean, store your chemicals safely and properly labeled. Allow your equipment to air dry. Pay attention to the details.

Another satisfactory cleaning solution for carboys and other equipment is ammonia. Mix a few tablespoons of unscented household ammonia with 2 gallons of water and your are ready to clean out your carboys.

All these solutions are much better than washing soda, which leaves a residue, which is difficult to remove.

BASIC WINE INFORMATION

Now that you are about to make wine, lets discuss some basic information After the grapes have been purchased, your equipment all sanitized; you're abou ready to watch nature at work, converting sugar into alcohol.

Weather its red or white or even blush wines, the grapes need to be crushec and the stems removed. Why must we crush the grapes you ask? Simply, tc allow the juice from inside the berry to come in contact with the yeast.

GRAPE YIELDS

How much wine do you intend to make?

➢ On the average it takes about 12-15 pounds of grape to make one galloi of wine.

Because of the crushing, pressing and fermentation techniques, you wil make more red wine than white from the same amount of grapes. A food grade plastic 55-gallon drum with the top cut off will hold about 450-500 pounds o. grape. Remember never to fill your primary fermentation container more thai 80% to allow the cap to rise. Usually a 55 drum used as a primary fermentatior container will hold about 11 boxes of grape.

Most California wine grapes are shipped in boxes that contain from 36 to 42 pounds of grapes depending on variety and the grower. If you buy direct from a local vineyard, you will probably be buying by the pound. Buy the freshest grape that you can find. Fresh wine juice is usually sold in 6-gallon plastic pails, whicł will eventually produce a bit more than 5 gallons of wine.

Growing up, it was not uncommon for my Grandfather to make 3 barrels oł red wine with a capacity of 40-50 gallons each. In addition, one barrel of white wine was made. When we went to buy grapes, we would fill a small dumptruck loaded with boxes of grapes. Weather your buying a few boxes of grape or 100 boxes, you will have to estimate your yield in order to have sufficient room for fermentation and storage.

MUST

The product produced from crushing and stemming the berries is called *MUST*. After crushing and stemming, the must contains about 80% juice, 16 % skins and the balance, 4% seeds. Most often, the color for red wines, *PIGMENT* comes from the skins of the berry. This is the reason for fermenting red wines with the skins in order to extract the red color we desire. The seeds contain about 70% of the tannins. Tannins are important for the aging and taste of our finished wines.

There are so many variations in winemaking for the contact time of the grape skins and seeds, particularly with red wines. This is a very important aspect of wine making. Shorter contact time between the skins, seeds and juices will usually give you a less tannic wine, while increased contact time will increase the tannin in your wine. From the same grape, many variations in flavor will occur just by changing the contact time. Heat and color extraction are also other important considerations that is discussed later. As a rough rule of thumb, shorter contact between juice and skins/seeds will give you a wine that can be drank earlier and longer contact will give you a more tannic wine that can age longer. Experiment, use the same grape, and shorten the contact time on one batch for early consumption. With the second batch, increase the contact time for extended aging and later consumption.

A word of advice from my experience. Over the years, I have found that the lower tannin wines are more suitable for the home winemaker if for no other reason, we can drink it sooner. I very much like heavy, intense reds but that can be obtained through grape selection rather than extended contact between juice and skins/seeds. Most home winemakers simply cannot store barrel after barrel of wine for years, waiting for the high tannin wines to mature. Every year, I do make some wine for extended aging, but for the most part, I believe most home made wines are consumed within 2 years of being made.

Since you do not usually ferment white wines in contact with their skin and seeds, contact time is not a question.

FERMENTATION HEAT

To understand what will be happening, you should understand what happens during fermentation. When you add yeast to the crushed grape, fermentation will begin. As the sugar is converted to alcohol, carbon dioxide and heat will be by-products of the fermentation process. If you are fermenting in closed containers, you will hear the carbon dioxide bubbling through your air lock. As you watch the cap rise in your fermentation container, you will see the bubbling of carbon dioxide. As a result, heat will also present. The formula for fermentation is:

Grape sugar + yeast = alcohol + Co2 + heat

Excessive heat will destroy wine yeast cells and stop fermentation. During fermentation, the temperature of the crushed grape must will rise about 2.3 degrees F for every 1- % drop in Brix.

As an example, if we start fermentation at 70 degrees F and the grape must has a starting sugar content of 22 Brix. The potential temperature rise of almost 51 degrees will result in a fermentation temperature of over 120 degrees. This will stop fermentation!

Winemakers must realize that wine yeast does begin to die at 100°F degrees. Remember to keep fermentation temperature under 100 degrees. For the home wine maker, these high fermentation temperatures usually will not be reached. Small fermentation containers dissipate the building heat and should not be a problem. We have used everything from 55 gallon plastic barrels to oak barrels and 55 gallon stainless steel containers and have never had a temperature problem. Check your fermentation temperatures every day particularly if you are not fermenting in a cool place such as a basement.

As a general rule of thumb, red wines are usually fermented at 70-90 degrees for 4-12 days. There is no exact temperature for fermenting, but try to stay in the mid to high 80's for red wines. White wines must be fermented at a cooler temperature from 55-70 degrees for 10-30 days. Keeping your white wine cool is very important in making quality white wines. I try to keep my white fermenting at about 65 degrees or less. If you're making wine in the basement as I do, maintaining a constant temperature is very easy.

Under normal conditions, yeast will continue working until all the sugar in the grape is converted to alcohol, up to about 15% alcohol. At 15% alcohol, the yeast will stop working leaving the balance of the sugar unfermented, also known as residual sugar. There are methods of fooling the yeast in order to obtain a bit higher alcohol and will be discussed later.

➢ Just as temperatures over 100 degrees will start to kill the yeast cells, temperatures below 50 degrees will also give you trouble. At these low temperatures yeast will grow very slow.

There are advanced techniques for the cold fermentation of white wines but generally, you will want higher temperatures, particularly with red wines where color extraction is wanted.

If your making wine in your basement, temperature should not be a major problem. It's nice to have a thermometer to check the temperature of your must. If the temperature is getting too high, plastic bags of ice can be placed into your must. If the temperature is too low, an electric blanket can be wrapped around your primary fermentation container to help raise the temperature a bit.

Most commercial wineries use stainless tanks that can be cooled or heated as need be. An older technique that is suitable for the home winemaker comes from France. The French use a coil called a *DRAPEAU* that is no more than stainless steel coil that is immersed into your vat of crushed grapes. Either hot or cold liquid is circulated through this coil to raise or lower the temperature. We have a stainless steel coil made from tubing that we place into our tanks. On each end is a plastic adapter, which we connect to garden hoses and connect to the kitchen faucet. Hot or cold water is run slowly through the coil to heat or cool. There are wort chillers available from beer making supply shops if you desire. Do not use any other metal besides stainless steel. Also, plastic does not effectively transfer heat.

COLOR EXTRACTION

There are 3 factors that effect the extraction of color from red skinned grapes. These factors are:

TIME

TEMPERATURE

ALCOHOL CONCENTRATION.

The skins of most all red varieties contain the pigment and some tannins. Most of the tannin is contained in the seeds. Usually the pulp of the grape contains no pigment. Color extraction is desired in red wines. Studies have shown the maximum extraction occurs during 3-5 days of skin contact. As your grape juice ferments and alcohol is produced, the alcohol assists in color extraction.

To insure maximum color extraction in red wines, fermentation temperatures should be in the range from 70 - 90 degrees F.

➢ Be sure to not allow your fermentation temperature go over 100 Degrees F since yeast cells will begin to die and fermentation will stop.

Another step in maximizing color extraction from red grapes is known as *punching down* the **cap**. You will notice when your wine must begins to ferment, the skins and seeds known as the **cap** will start to rise. This *CAP* will comprise about 30% of the volume. As the cap begins to rise, you will punch down the cap twice a day.

For small fermentation containers (up to 55 gallons or so), simply wash and sanitize your arms, and push the floating cap, skins and seeds, down further in your container. The object is to mix the floating cap with the free run juice under the cap Do this twice a day. Larger scale winemakers pump the liquid from the bottom of the fermentation container over the cap, thus sinking the cap.

I started using a hand dry wall mixer to punch down the cap. This mixer looks similar to a potato masher but only larger with a wooden handle. These are available at dry wall supply houses. The benefit of using the mixer is that's its much easier to sanitize and you don't get your shirt all stained as you punch down the cap while realizing your late for work.

Since we are not looking for any skin color with white wines, color extraction is not of concern.

MAKING YOUR WINE

Basic equipment list for first 5-gallon batch of wine.

- Hydrometer
- 2-5 gallon glass carboys
- 2- bored rubber stopper
- 2- plastic air lock
- 6 feet plastic tubing
- 1- small plastic funnel
- 1- cork inserting tool
- 25 corks
- 1- package of campden tablets or potassium metabisulfite
- 1- 5 gram package of wine yeast

Fresh wine grapes (about 80 pounds) or 6-gallon pail of grape juice

Small batch of juice fermenting

CRUSHING THE GRAPES

STEP ONE

For just about all wines, the grapes must be crushd in order to release the juice. Whether you will be removing the grapes from the stems by hand, the way my Great Grandfather and I did it or use a modern crusher-stemmer now is the time to crush the grapes. First I'll explain the process for making red wines, and then explain whites and roses.

By now, you've decided whether to make red, white or a rose wine. All these grape types must be crushed. After you have selected the best grapes and brought your grapes home, let's crush. Before you start to crush, wash and sanitize all your equipment. This includes your crusher and primary fermentation container or your feet if you're planning to use the original grape crush method, which is simply stomping the grape with your feet, in a clean container.

A modern crusher-stemmer is placed over your barrel and crushes the grape and at the same time removes the grape from the stem, discarding the stem. These at quite expensive but are available through many wine making supply houses. By removing the stem, your wine will be less tannic. This is a lesson I learned from my Great Grandfather who removed the grape from the stem by hand. This was his secret to great wine.

Although it is now a well-known fact that fermenting the crushed grapes with the stems produces a highly tannic and astringent wine, in years past, this was not known. Most of the old amateur winemakers fermented the grapes with the stems.

For many years I used a plain crusher and it is also placed over your barrel. It simply crushes the grape leaving the stem as it is. A little trick to remove the stems is get a piece of 1x3 pine about 4 feet long, put about 20 10 penny nails in the last foot of the board. You pull the stem remover through your container and remove the stems. Using this stem remover is a lot of work when doing several barrels of grape must. For smaller amounts, this works very well.

Many wine grape sellers will crush, stem and press your fresh grapes for a minimal charge. This is a good way to get started in winemaking and save the equipment expense.

Now you might ask, how big of a primary fermentation container do I need? Well, to begin, you will need an open container about 25% larger than your volume of crushed grape. This will allow for the cap to rise without spilling out of the primary fermentation barrel. I use food grade; 55-gallon plastic drums with the top cut off for primary fermentation. On these drums, we drilled a hole and installed a 1inch plastic shut off valve about 3 inches from the bottom for removing the free run juice after fermentation. The 55-gallon drum will hold about 11 boxes of grapes, which is about 400-450 pounds. With this amount, you will wind up with about 130-140 bottles of wine.

➢ As a rough guide, you can expect to make a gallon of wine from 12 to 15 pounds of grape.

I don't recommend using wood barrels for the primary fermentation. This usually leads to trouble since the open barrel can never be cleaned and sanitized well enough. For hundreds of years, wood barrels were used for primary fermentation, but personally, I rather use plastic or stainless steel.

Stainless steel drums and containers are excellent primary fermentation containers. You can purchase stainless steel wine storage tanks from some winemaking supply house's. These stainless tanks have variable seal lids which can be used to store your wine later on. These come in plastic and stainless and the sizes range from 50 liters to 500 liters, ideally suited for the home wine maker.

The **crush** or as it known in France as *Foulage* is a fun time for us. We always have a wine crush party. After all our equipment has been cleaned and sanitized, the grapes crushed and tested, everything cleaned up, we break out some of last years wine. Someone picks up fresh Italian bread from the old bakery, we bring fresh mozzarella, provolone, dried salami's, olives and anything else we might need such as lots of wine. We talk about improvements we might make to our recipes to solving the world's problems to how much we over-paid for the grape. Invite a few friends to help, its better than a football game and you get to enjoy great company, food and of course wine.

Both red and white wines are crushed in this manner. Both are left to sit on the skins overnight.

After the grape crush or ***pigiatura*** be sure to loosely cover your primary fermentation tanks with plastic or cheesecloth to keep out the fruit fly's and dirt. But before you cover your must, be sure to add sulfites. This is discussed next.

If you are buying grape juice, you will be skipping the crushing step. You will open the pail of juice, measure the Brix, acid and pH and proceed to step two.

Crusher Destemmer on top of Plastic Barrel, ready to crush or *pigiatura*

ADDING SULFITES

STEP TWO

After crushing the grape, you will add sulfite. This is to stop unwanted wild yeast growth and oxidation. Don't be overly concerned about adding sulfide to your wine must, its been done for hundreds of years and protects the wine. It is well documented that the Romans mentioned using sulfur for the preservation of wine.

How much do I add? Well, for red wines, I look to add about 50ppm and white wine about 70ppm. The white wines needs extra protection against oxidation, which will leave your white wine dark and brown.

The sulfide, **SO2,** is added to the must as soon as it's crushed. Potassium Metabisulfite powder is available at wine supply shop. A with all chemicals, follow the manufacturers label instructions. A Metabisulfite solution can also be used as a sanitizing solution for your wine equipment. Add about 50ppm of potassium Metabisulfite powder to your must, this is about 1/4 teaspoon per 5 gallons. As a rough estimate, 1/4 teaspoon of Potassium Metabisulfite weighs about 1.5 grams, a teaspoon will weigh about 6.2 grams and a tablespoon will hold about 20.0 grams.

Also available are Campden tablets that you can obtain at wine supply shops. Campden tablets are pre-measured in tablets containing about .44 grams of sulfite, which is enough for 1 gallon of must. You will need 5 tablets for 5 gallons of must. These tablets must be crushed prior to adding to your must For the beginner, use the campden tablets and follow the manufacturers label instructions.

Be sure to mix the sulfide throughout the must. You will add the yeast to your must in about 24 hours.

➤ Never add sulfur to wines when they are still fermenting. This may affect wine flavor adversely.

SULFUR DIOXIDE

Just as a reminder, Potassium Metabisulfite is about 57% SO2. 1/4 teaspoon per 5 gallons of wine will give you about 40-45 PPM of SO2. Always read and follow the manufacturers instructions.

Campden Tablets contains about 48% SO2. One tablet per gallon of wine will give you about 75ppm of SO2 in your wine. These tablets must be crushed before adding to your wine.

➤ For red wines, I look to add about 50ppm and white wine about 70ppm.

The following will give you an idea on how much Potassium Metabisulfite powder per gram.

Amount	1 gallon	**5 Gallon**	50 gallons
1 Gram	150 PPM	**30 PPM**	3 PPM

The following will give you an estimate for 1/4 teaspoon of Potassium Metabisulfite powder.

Amount	1 gallon	**5 gallons**
¼ teaspoon (1.5 grams)	225 PPM	**45 PPM**

Always read and follow the manufacturer's instructions.

ADDING YEAST

STEP THREE

Some winemakers still today, depend on wild yeast. Most wild yeast's wi only tolerate 4-8% alcohol before dying off. To insure full fermentation, believe its much better to use one of the active dried wine yeast that is availabl at most wine supply shops. Wine yeasts are not the same as baker's yeast; sc please do not use baker's yeast to ferment your wine.

My Grandfather and Great Grandfather never added commercial yeast, no do I think commercial yeast was available. As with commercial wineries year ago and to a very limited extent today depended solely upon wild yeast. The wild yeast was found in wine cellars, in the barrels and on the grapes naturally in the vineyard.

These wild yeast strains range from excellent, which are the bases for the commercially available wine yeast to very poor. The poor strains of yeast would not fully ferment the sugars found in the grape and some gave off flavors.

Many types of wine yeasts are available to the home winemaker. There are yeasts for red and white wine, champagne and sherry and the names vary depending on the manufacturer. All the yeast used for winemaking is known scientifically as *Saccharomyces*.

Most active wine yeasts are packed in sealed 5-gram envelopes; similar tc dried bread yeast. Each envelope is sufficient yeast for 5 gallons of must or juice.

➢ Do **NOT** pour the dried yeast directly into your grape must or juice Yeast must be rehydrated first.

To insure proper rehydration, pour the dried yeast into a cup of warm, abou 102 degrees F, NOT HOT water. Wait about 30-60 minutes, and then stir. You will see the yeast starting to foam. You can now pour the rehydrated yeast intc your must or juice. Since the yeast is a living organism, the yeast will multiply ir your wine must, converting sugar into alcohol. Remember; wine yeast dies off a about 104 degrees.

Add your yeast about 24 hours after crushing and sulfiting your must. Rec wine will stay in the primary fermentation container for 3-5 days for color extraction. White wines will stay on the skins for 24 hours and then be pressed. I will discuss white wines after going through the process for reds.

➢ Adding the rehydrated yeast o the grape juice/must is called *inoculation*.

TYPES OF YEAST

There are many types of wine yeast, many of which are used to produce certain characteristic in finished wine. The following charts give you an idea if the various types of yeast available at the winemaking supply shop or catalog.

LAVIN YEAST

Company	Yeast Name	Wine Style	Alcohol	Character	Temp Range F
Lavin	71-B-1122	All	14%	Softens taste Fruity	58-85
Lavin	RC 212	Dry White Blush, Reds	14%	Improve Mouthfeel	58-85
Lavin	KIV-1116	General	16%	Stuck Ferment	58-85
Lavin	EC-1118	Champagne Late Season	18%	Strong Fermenter	45-95
Lavin	D-47	Chardonnay Rose	14%	Good Mouthfeel	50-85

RED STAR YEAST

Company	Yeast Name	Wine Style	Alcohol	Character	Temp Range F
Red Star	Pasteur Red	Reds	16%	Fruity Reds	64-86
Red Star	Montrachet	Reds	13%	Intense Reds	60-86
Red Star	Pasteur Champagne	Dry Whites	13-15%	White, stuck Fermentation	60-86
Red Star	Premier Cuvee	All but high sugar	18%	All, stuck Ferment	44-95
Red Star	Cote des Blanc	Fruity Whites	12-14%	Fruity Whites	64-86

White Labs

Company	Yeast Name	Wine Style	Alcohol	Character	Temp Range F
White Labs	Champagne	Champagne	17%	Sparkling	70-75
White Labs	Chardonnay	White Wine	14%	Fruity	50-90
White Labs	Merlot	Red Wine	18%	Ferments Dry	60-90
White Labs	Cabernet	Red Wine	16%	Full body Reds	60-90

WYEAST YEAST

Company	Yeast Name	Wine Style	Alcohol	Character	Temp Range F
Wyeast	Bordeaux	Reds	14%	Rich Flavor	55-90
Wyeast	Pasteur Red	Reds	14%	Full Body	55-90
Wyeast	Rudisheimer	German Whites, Ice	12-13%	Fruity, rich Flavor	55-74
Wyeast	Pasteur Champagne	Dry whites Champagne	17%	Dry white	55-74
Wyeast	Eau de Vie	Grappa Cordials	21%	Clean	65-80

DURING PRIMARY FERMENTATION OF RED WINE

STEP FOUR-RED WINE

This step is skipped for white wine, go directly to step—pressing

Within 24 hours of adding your yeast you will notice that fermentation is starting. The grape skins are starting to rise to the top and you'll notice small bubbles escaping, this is **Carbon Dioxide**. In Italian, this is known as **Bollitura** or when the wine starts to boil. Carbon dioxide along with heat and alcohol are the result of fermentation. Allowing the skins to soak with the juice is known as **maceration**.

The layer of grape that rises to the top of your wine is known as the *CAP*. In Italian the cap is *Capello* and in France, the cap is known as the *Chapeau*.

This **CAP** will comprise about 30% of the volume. As the cap begins to rise, you will punch down the cap twice a day.

The hard cap with the tool I use to punch the cap

The purpose of punch down the cap is to maximize color extraction from red grapes. You will notice, as your wine must begins to ferment, the skins and seeds, known, as the cap will start to rise. For small fermentation containers (up to 55 gallons or so), simply wash and sanitize your arms, and push the floating

43

cap, skins and seeds, down further in your container. The object is to mix the floating cap with the free run juice under the cap. Do this twice a day. Larger scale winemakers can pump the liquid from the bottom of the fermentation container over the cap, thus sinking the cap.

In addition to the color extraction, the addition of oxygen by punching down the cap improves fermentation.

When to press your crushed grapes? This aspect of winemaking can vary greatly. Some deep, intense red wine is left on the skin for up to 30 days while the surface of the must is covered by carbon dioxide.

➤ For the home wine maker, 3 to 8 days of skin contact prior to pressing should be sufficient time for color extraction.

Take readings of the must's sugar content daily with your hydrometer. Once you get below 5 Brix, its time to press your red grapes. I prefer pressing my wine a bit sooner than later to allow the wine to complete primary fermentation in the carboy or stainless steel tank. Over, the years, I've experimented by splitting my batch, pressing the must before and after the 5 Brix point. You will taste variations of the finished wine. This is part of the art of winemaking.

➤ Remember, if you want a lighter, fruitier red wine, ferment on the skins a shorter period. 3-4 days. If you want to make a richer, full-bodied wine, allow the grape must to macerate longer. 5-8 days

Many old time wine makers stuck to the hard rule of 7 days contact time before pressing. The stems were not removed and they usually wound up with a very harsh, tannic wine. I don't recommend this method. Use your hydrometer, take Brix readings daily and press the must when the sugar level gets to about 1-5% Brix.

➤ Press your grape when the must goes below 5 brix.

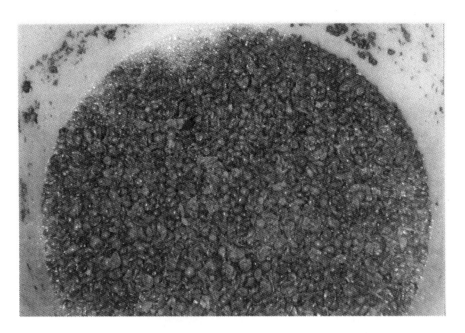

Notice the CO2 bubbles during active fermentation

PRESSING

STEP FIVE

The reason for pressing is simply to separate the wine from the seeds and skin. This is known as *Pressurage* in French. After your primary fermentation of your red grape in your open container and you've punched the cap down twice a day for the past 3-5 days, you're ready to press the must.

> ➢ Do Not Punch the cap down on the day you plan to press the must

Remember that red wines are pressed after fermentation while white wine is fermented after pressing. White grapes are crushed; sulfur dioxide added, allowed to sit over night and pressed the next day. Yeast is added after the pressing with white wines. White wine juice is then placed into carboys, airlock on top and fermented till dry.

By now, you will have noticed that the skins are thin, and there is a lot of juice under the cap. The juice under the cap is known as *free run juice*. The free run juice under the cap is usually about 60-70% of the juice. The free run juice usually makes the best wines being superior with less tannin than pressed juice. You can either keep these free run juices separate from the pressed juice or blend them together as I do. Again, this is the art, part of your personal taste.

To remove the free run juice is a simple matter if you installed either a drain valve (food grade plastic) or bung at the bottom of your primary fermentation container. Simply open the valve and let it flow into a clean sanitized pail.

From the pail, your free run juice is transferred into your carboys or barrels. Be sure to sanitize your funnels.

Once all the free run juice is drained off, its time to begin pressing. Before you start, be sure to wash, rinse and sanitize your press. With your clean pail, start transferring the remaining must into the press. There are several types of presses but most home winemakers will be using a basket press that pushes the must down into a cylinder made of wood slats or a stainless steel cylinder. After assembling the press, begin pressing. Press slowly, more is extracted when pressure is applied slowly allowing the juices to flow. You will not extract every drop of juice but many old timers tried very hard. After pressing once, they would release the pressure, fluff up the *pomace* and press it again to extract a bit more wine. This routine can continue 24 hours, allowing the press to drip wine over night. I don't. One good pressing is good enough. The seeds and skins remaining after pressing are called **pommace or press cake or Vinnace.**

Red juice flowing from my Grandfather's press or *Torchio*

SECONDARY FERMENTATION FOR REDS

STEP SIX

After pressing, you can keep the free juice separate or combine the press juice with the free run juice for secondary fermentation. The juice will be put into carboys, barrels or adjustable lid tanks, leaving some air space on top. I do not wait till primary fermentation has used all the sugar, I like to press prior to totally dry, usually at 1-5 Brix. This insures that carbon dioxide is still being produced strongly, and I find it much better for the health of the wine.

With white wines, there will be no free run, as all the grape are pressed within 24 hours of crushing, with SO2 added when you crushed the whites.

Once you've just about filled your carboys or tanks, put the airlock with rubber stopper on top to prevent contamination from air. Within a few weeks, fermentation will slow, and then stop completely. Until this time, your wine has been cloudy and murky. The wine will start to clear, the dead yeast cells settling to the bottom.

Within 30 days or so, its time for the first racking.

Wine during secondary fermentation

48

RACKING

STEP SEVEN, EIGHT and NINE

Racking is an important step in wine making. One of the purposes for RACKING is to clarify your wine. During racking. You will be removing the clear wine from the sediment or **gross lees** from the bottom of your carboy or barrel. Another aspect during racking, is the aeration of your wine, which helps to form flavor compounds and reducing any excess sulfur. The sediment that is found in this wine is called gross lees.

This first racking is known as **Svinare** in Italian. In France, the term for racking is *soutirage.*

Let's discuss red wines first. When do I rack? The first time to rack your red wine is shortly after fermentation stops. I try to rack as soon as I can. If your using glass carboys, clean and sanitize your extra carboy that you will be racking into. Next, elevate you wine filled container without shaking. Red wine should not be left on the gross lees for any longer than necessary. I usually rack the first time within one month that fermentation has stopped.

Now, it's simply a matter of siphoning (or pumping) from one container into another. The objective is to leave the sediment on the bottom. I still hear my grandfather's voice as I helped him, NO SHAKE! Do not stir up the sediment. We are trying to clarify the wine. Don't worry if you stir it up a bit, you'll be racking again. Again, be sure to fill the container up to the top with little air space. You might have to use wine from another container to do so; put air is now the enemy of wine. Remember to add sulfite as you rack at the rate recommended by the manufacturer.

The second racking is usually in early spring, late February or early March. The wine has had time to settle and cold stabilize which is discussed later. Again, add sulfide, and try to cleanly remove the wine from the sediment. Some people and commercial operations use filters, but I believe, you remove some essence and character from the wine if you filter red wines. Taking your time, you can usually finish with a perfectly clear red wine without filtering. Again, fill your container, leaving hardly any air space, which is less than 1 inch in a carboy.

Over the winter, if you allow your wine to get to about 30 degrees, wine will undergo what is called cold stabilization.

During the time period between the first and second racking, a naturally occurring reaction takes place. This chemical reaction is **called** *Cold Stabilization.* When wine goes below 32 degrees for several weeks, bitartrate is precipitated. This bitartrate is tartaric acid also know as cream of tarter.

After the wine is cold stabilized, you will notice crystals that will have settled to the bottom of your tank or carboys. These crystals are not harmful but do not look very nice at the bottom of your wine once it has been bottled. These crystal's help to seal the gross lees, making the second or third racking a bit easier. The second and third rackings are known as *Travasare* in Italian.

With the wine cellar we use, cold stabilization comes easy. This concrete room was built by my Grandfather just for winemaking. We simply open the one small vent window and the temperature drops to whatever winter temperature we are having here in NJ. If you live in an area that does not get cold enough or don't have access to such a wine cellar, you have do the same by placing your carboys in an old refrigerator.

> ➢ The benefits from cold stabilization are that the acid is reduced abit but more importantly, your wine has a softer, more pleasant mouthfeel.

The last racking, usually, is just prior to bottling. We usually rack a final time, and bottle the same day. I've had wines that were perfectly clear after the first racking and others that needed 4-5 rackings or other that just won't clear.

At times, you will have to add something in order to clarify the wine so that your wine falls brilliantly clear.

Racking from primary fermentation container

TYPICAL RACKING SCHEDULE

First Racking	Within 30 days after primary fermentation
Second Racking	2-3 months after - Christmas
Third Racking	3 months later- Spring time

BOTTLING

STEP TEN

I highly recommend bottling your wine. Many old timers, such as my grandfather would keep aging his wine in oak barrels until it was needed. At that point, we would siphon the wine from the wood barrel into glass carboys. Remember to leave as little air space as possible, as air is an enemy of wine. After the carboys were filled and corked, the wine was ready. Every night before dinner, my grandfather would fill a bottle to be consumed during dinner. If I ate over, it was my job, to go fill the wine bottle. I was only 10 years old or so, and I loved the job very much.

He did have one condition when I went to the wine cellar to fill the wine; he wanted me to whistle, your wondering why? Well, he thought I would only stop whistling for a second or two in order to start siphoning the wine from the carboy. Well, as you might figure, to this day, I still can't whistle, must be a mental block.

You can go buy all your wine bottles if you like, which does add extra expense to your winemaking costs. I'm far from a save the earth type person, but for wine bottles, I recycle. Start saving your empty bottles, ask your friends and relatives to start saving. I wash each bottle, remove the label and store them wherever I can find room. Its best to initially clean them as you go on, otherwise, it's an enormous job. Once the word gets out you need wine bottles; you'll have more than enough. How many times, I've found a case or two of empty bottles at my door upon returning home. Not all the bottles are useable, I get screw top bottles (which I don't use), gallon jugs, you name it. The ones I don't need, well, recycle at the curb.

My winemaking friend, George F. Talarico, who was retired, would collect large amounts of bottles. Very often, he would lunch with A NJ State Senator. To the Senator's, embarrassment, after lunch, George would collect the empty wine bottles from the rear of the restaurant and load them in the senator's car. Most restaurants are happy to give you all the empty wine bottles you want.

Before I go on, I should mention that great friendships are made by winemaking. I met George F. Talarico long ago on jury duty. Although he was much older than myself, we became good friends over the years with him being a research chemist and in charge of regulatory affairs and myself a food inspector. Although he passed away a few years ago, his memory is alive in the wine cellar with me.

I was already making wine so I brought George a few bottles to try. He loved it and fondly remembered how he would help his father and uncles make wine. I invited him to come make wine together. Over the years, our wine improved with George's understanding of chemistry. I learned far more than just chemistry from George, he was a great man. His accomplishments go on and on and include having been awarded a Silver Star and 2 bronze stars in action in Europe during World War 2. It was with he and his brother in law, Rudy Riccardi that we named our wine, **I Tres Pescadori**, for the 3 fisherman. While we were not making wine together, we would fish and crab together at the Jersey Shore.

Between George and myself, we would drive Rudy crazy, continually telling him something was not clean enough.

Use only, clean bottle, and be selective. Wash and sanitize your bottles before use. I usually clean 5-6 bottles at a time, placing them in a 5-gallon pail with 1/4 cup of bleach. Let the bottles soak overnight, it makes removing the labels very easy, in fact, most come right off. When you're actually just about to bottle, we sanitize and rinse the bottles again, just prior to filling. If you look in your wine supply shop, you'll find faucet adapters, which allow you to spray hot water from your faucet into bottles or carboys, while holding the bottle upside down, so the bottle drains as you wash.

Also available are bottle sanitizers. Bottle sanitizers are a simple pump that contains a reservoir of sanitizing solution that squirts sanitizer into your bottle as you press the bottle over the pump. After the bottle is sanitized, it's rinsed with clean water and place to drain. We use a bottle tree, which holds about 90 bottles upside down, for proper drainage. Be sure to fully drain your bottles after cleaning and before storing them. Bottles than have been rinsed out and not fully drained will produce mold on the inside of the bottle. Be sure to rinse and allow your bottles to drain till dry.

Your now ready to bottle. For those who want to know the actually names and volume of different type wine bottles, see the chart below.

> ➤ When bottling, be sure to fill the bottle to the proper level. The bottle should be filled so that ½ inch of air space is between the bottom of the cork and the level of the wine.

When we bottle our wine, this is usually a lot of fun. Our quality control team (either George, Joe or myself) personally guarantees that every bottle is filled to the exact point to leave a ½ inch headspace. Now if the bottle is slightly over filled, our designated quality control person, or whoever wants a sip, must sip the bottle to bring the level down to the proper level. This then is a major problem, causing the bottle to be underfilled. Now, if we've filled too many bottles that afternoon, this can happen several times before the level is just right.

Fluid Ounces	Bottle Name	Metric Liters
6.3	Split	187ml
12.7	Half Bottle	375m
25.4	Bottle	750ml
50.7	Magnum	1.5l
101.4	Double Magnum	3l
135.2	Jug	4l
152.2	Rehoboam	4.5l
202.9	Methuselah	6l
304.5	Samanazar	9l
405.8	Balthazar	12l
507.2	Nebuchadnezar	15l

CORKING THE BOTTLES

STEP ELEVEN

The final step to your winemaking is bottling the wine. In order to use corks, you will have to buy a corker. They range in price from 20 dollars for a small hand operated model to about 100 dollars for a floor model and up to thousands of dollars.

Most 750-ml wine bottles use a number 9 cork. You can get corks in 1 ½ or 1-¾ inch lengths. They say the longer corks can keep the wine longer. I've never had the problem of long-term storage of my wine; our biggest problem is running out of wine. Some of the European bottles use a number 8-size cork, which is a bit smaller. Also available are the newer synthetic corks that also do a nice job but seem a bit more difficult to insert and remove.

For any of the corks, you will need a corker to insert them in the bottle. If using a small hand corked, I found it much easier to soak the corks in hot water mixed with 50ppm sulfide. After soaking in hot water, the corks being softened do go in easier.

> ➢ If using a hand corker, corks are much easier to insert if you place your corks in a large bowl of water and heat in the microwave for 5 minutes or so.

When corking, be sure to fill the bottle to the proper level. The cork should be level to the top of the bottle and the bottle filled so that ½ inch of air space is between the bottom of the cork and the level of the wine.

> ➢ After bottling, I usually put the bottles in a cardboard wine box, and allow the bottles to sit upright for about a week. This allows the pressure inside the bottle to equalize.

After one week, you can put a plastic, heat shrinkable neckband capsules on the top of your corked bottle. This is not needed but does add a nice finished look to your wine. These capsules are available in a wide range of colors from many wine supply catalogs and shops. They sell special heaters to heat shrink on the top of the wine bottle, but a hand held hair dryer can work if only doing a few.

WINE AGEING

Wine aging is an important aspect of wine enjoyment.

Spectacular changes can occur to fine wines allowed to age. Several important factors must be considered before deciding to age wine.

1. Can the wine be stored properly with correct temperatures and humidity?
2. Can wine be protected from air contact?
3. Is the wine capable of improving with age?

To begin, most white and blush wines do not improve with age. These wines are best drunk within 1 to 2 years of being made.

The wines made from following grape types usually benefit from aging. Also shown is the number of years that these wines can be stored in the bottle.

RED GRAPE

GRAPE TYPE	YEARS
Merlot	2-10
Cabernet Sauvignon	4-20
Pinot Noir	2-8
Shiraz/ Syrah	4-6
Sangiovese	2-8
Zinfandel	2-6

WHITE GRAPE

GRAPE TYPE	YEARS
Riesling	2-30
Chardonnay	2-6

BOTTLE AGING

Since most home winemakers do not have the room for extensive barrel o carboy aging, we are limited to bottle aging. Over the years, we have very successfully bottle aged many of our wines, and they continue to get better Wines can be aged too long, loosing color and flavor but very honestly, ou problem has never been excessive quantities of wine but rather having drank it al before the problem of loosing quality.

➤ Never store partially filled carboys or barrels of wine. During fermentation, air is a friend to the must, but once fermentation i complete, air is an enemy to wine.

Be sure to store your bottles of wine on their sides so that the cork stay moist. Occasionally check the bottle corks for any mold growth or leakers. Mos importantly, it is your duty and obligation to continually check the aging proces by tasting the wine.

The one point you should remember is that the smaller the container, the faster wine ages. A carboy ages faster than a barrel and a single bottle ages faste than a carboy. Secondly, wine likes a stable temperature for storage. A coo place in your basement should be perfect, try to maintain your wine at 50-60 degrees. Wine should be kept away from sunlight.

From the moment wine is made, wine is constantly changing, until the poin that the wine is just too old to drink. This may take as few as 3 or 4 years for a white wine and up to 30-40 years for a deep intense red wine. Red wines las much longer, taking longer to mature because of the tannins found naturally ir reds. The aging process can be seen in color changes during the life of a wine Below is a chart that explains the color changes through the aging process.

RED WINES

Fresh	Young	Mature	Aged	Old	Dead
Purple Plum	Ruby Cherry	Red Strawberry	Mahogany Garnet	Tawny	Brown

WHITE WINES

Fresh	Young	Mature	Aged	Old	Dead
Pale Greenish	Pale Straw	Yellow	Golden	Amber	Brown

STEPS FOR MAKING RED WINE

CRUSH-DESTEM
Add Sulfur Dioxide
Adjust acid/sugar
Wait 24 Hours ADD YEAST Inoculation
FERMENT 4-10 Days
PRESS After fermentation stops SETTLE-RACK Add sulfur dioxide
COLD STABILIZE Over winter
RACK 2nd TIME Early spring
RACK 3rd TIME if needed **Add sulfur**
BOTTLE Age in bottle

WHITE WINES

The process for making white wine is very similar to making reds. Actually, in some parts of Europe, very hearty full-bodied whites are made exactly as the reds. The grape is crushed and allowed to sit on the skin to fully ferment. My grandfather made his white wine, a Muscat in this manner. The wine was never clear or light yellow but more of a clear brown. The flavor was intense but the color turns off a lot of people.

WHITE WINES

As I said before, I find high quality white wines much harder to make. As a beginner, I would recommend making a red wine. But, after you have made a few good red wines, lets try a white.

CRUSH THE GRAPES

Just as with reds, you will crush and destem the white grapes.

➤ At this point you will be sure to add your sulfite to about 70ppm.

White wines needs extra protection against oxidation, which will leave your white wine dark and brown.

Now at this point, you can cold soak the crushed grape overnight or press immediately. These are two different methods but I prefer to press immediately, within 2-3 hours. Just after crushing, I add Pectic Enzymes to help break down the grape tissue and release more juice. Follow the manufactures label directions for amount to add per gallon of must. If you ferment the free run juice separate from the pressed juice, I add about 1 gram of grape tannin per 4 gallons of free run juice. If you ferment the free run juicewith the pressed juice, tannin is not needed. You should try to get the temperature down to 50 degrees or so. In our area, the outdoor temperature is always warm when we buy the white grapes, but our supplier refrigerates his grape, which helps. In addition, we freeze 1gallon plastic jugs full of water, these frozen, sealed jugs are dropped into the must to keep the temperature down during the cold soak. Cold soaking helps retain the fruitiness to the wine and extracts a bit more flavor.

➤ White wines should be fermented at a cooler temperature to maintain fruitiness.

After allowing the white grape to cold soak from 8 to 24 hours, now is the time to press the grape. Although you crushed and destemed your grape, its easier to press the white grape if some stems are added to the crushed grape, other wise the skins pop out of the press.

Once you finish pressing, pour the juice into your carboy or tanks. Now you will let the juice settle for 24 hours, allowing the particles to settle. You will waste some juice, but the finished product is much better. After 24 hours, you will rack the juice into another carboy, leaving the thin, fluffy settlement behind. If you want, this too can be fermented, but keep it separate.

After racking you now add your yeast to the must Again, this is called inoculation. Follow the direction from this point on, same as red wine.

White wine during initial fermentation

STEPS FOR MAKING WHITE and BLUSH WINES

CRUSH-DESTEM
Add Sulfur Dioxide Add PECTIC ENZYME Adjust acid/sugar
PRESS ALLOW to SETTLE 24 hours RACK OFF SETTLEMENT
ADD YEAST Inoculation
FERMENT After fermentation stops SETTLE-RACK Add sulfur dioxide
COLD STABILIZE Over winter
RACK 2nd TIME Early spring
RACK 3rd TIME if needed **Add sulfur**
BOTTLE ENJOY

➤ An important point for making quality white wines is that air hurts white wines. While racking, do not splash the white wine into the carboy, but rather allow the siphon hose to sit in the wine that is in the carboy that you are racking into. Treat your white wines gently.

> Keep air away from your white wines. If you can fill the carboy witl carbon dioxide or nitrogen gas prior to racking into.

ROSE or BLUSH WINES

To make true rose such as white zinfandel or white grenache, both of whicl are very good, you will use red grapes. With most red grapes, only the skin i dark, with the juice being clear. Some rose wines are no more than white win with a bit of red wine added, but that is not a true rose.

Again, just as with reds and whites, you will crush the red grape. At thi point you will be sure to add your sulfite to about 50ppm. Allow the grapes to si on the skins for a few hours and your ready to press. The grapes should b pressed almost immediately after crushing in order to minimize color extraction Continue as you would whites, adding your yeast and your set. The juice shoulc be kept cool during fermentation to maintain fruitiness.

Most of the rose wines such as white Zinfandel or white Grenache are no totally dry. They have ½ to 1 ½ percent residual sugar. Since home winemaker do not have the filtration systems that large wineries have to stop fermentation we will ferment this wine dry. After racking, we will sweeten this wine. Pleas read the section on sweetening your wine.

If you want, you can press the must ever so slightly, getting a few gallons o juice for rose but leaving the remainder to fully ferment as a red. You will have to remove the must from your press and put it back into your primary fermentation container. The red wine you make will be very highly concentrate in color and taste.

Now you have the skins in the press, still with lots of color and taste. Witl these skins, I would make aquadde or second wine. Please read AQUADDE WINE, PIQUETTE, SUGAR or SECOND WINE.

ADJUSTING BRIX

Red grapes should have about 20 to 24 degrees Brix. White wines as well as blush wines grapes would contain 19 to 23 Brix. Sparkling wine grapes would have from 18 to 20 degrees Brix. This is only a guideline. I prefer my wines on the higher end on the scale. If your grape is a bit low in sugar or degrees Brix consider adding sugar. The brix if found to be too low should be adjusted prior to fermentation. At the back of the book is a chart on how much sugar is needed to raise the must in degrees brix. To add sugar is called **Chaptalization** or sugar **Amelioration**. Very roughly, you will add about ¼ cup of sugar to each gallon of must to raise one degree. Please look at the chart at the end of this book.

ADJUSTING ACID

Acid should be between 0.6% to 0.85%. For red wines, start with 0.65% acid and with white wines; start with 0.70% acid. Wine with less than 0.6% acid taste flat to most people and wines with over 0.9% have too much acid for enjoyable consumption.

Low acids wines are flat tasting and usually are short lived. Raising the acid on your wine juice/must is very easy. There are several acid blends on the market that contain tartaric, malic and citric acids.

More often we find high acid wine juice/must. Acid can only be reduced by small percentages. By adding too much chemical the taste can be changed. There are several ways of lowering acidity. One of the better ways is to inoculate your must with malolactic culture during fermentation. Follow the manufactures directions. Malolactic fermentation converts the harsh malic acid into the softer lactic acid. Malolactic fermentation adds a slight buttery taste to your wine.

Of course, cold stabilization will lower the acid some by precipitating some of the tartaric acid from the wine.

If you wine juice/must still must be reduced use Calcium Carbonate also known as precipitated chalk. Mix 2.6 grams per gallon of must to lower the acidity of the must by about 0.1%.

At times, you wind up with a finished wine that still has too much acid. In that case use Potassium Bicarbonate. Mix 3.4 grams per gallon of must to reduce acidity by about 0.1%.

➤ With both Potassium Carbonate and Calcium Carbonate never try to lower the total acid by more than .2%. If you do so, you can reduce the tartaric acid levels so low that your wine is flabby.

There is one last method to reducing the acid of the juice/must. You will make sugar syrup with water containing the same brix as your juice/must. If your must is 22 brix, you will have to add enough sugar to the water so that this syrup is 22 brix. For each gallon of must, prepare 1 pint of water with the sugar. You will then add about 1 1/4 pints of this syrup to each gallon of must. This will also lower the acid by 0.1% but will lessen the wines natural intensity some.

ADJUSTING pH

Most table wines, pH, should be between 3 and 4. If the pH of the grape juice is above 3.40, tartaric acid should be added to reduce the pH to between 3.25-3.40. When the pH of must is below 3.5, the wine will ferment much more evenly. It is better to leave your must alone if the acid is satisfactory but the pH is a bit off.

Grape juice/must that have a pH 3.0 and under are hard to start fermenting. If the must goes over pH of 4.0, the resulting wine will be flabby. We usually use pH test strips to test for pH. Follow the directions on the bottle. These test strips are very inexpensive.

ADVANCED EQUIPMENT

- ➢ Acid Test Kit
- ➢ Grape Press
- ➢ Crush-destemer
- ➢ Sulfur test kit
- ➢ Bottle sanitizer
- ➢ Bottle rack or tree
- ➢ Bottle rinser
- ➢ Carboy brushes
- ➢ Thermometer
- ➢ pH test strips
- ➢ Oak chips
- ➢ Capsuler or heat shrinker

Grape or fruit Press

Although, there is not better feeling than filling your press with grapes, the expense of a press is not for everyone.   Presses range in size from 30-pound capacity up to five hundred pound capacity. There are many variations.

Basket Press

The most common press for the home winemaker is the basket press. This style has been around for hundreds of years, my press that was my grandfathers was originally bought used. The baskets are traditionally made from oak wood slats, but you are now seeing the baskets made on stainless steel. The stainless steel basket type can be very expensive but are better adapted to pressing white grapes. Either red or white wine can be made with either the oak or stainless baskets. Basket presses are tightened by hand power, using a bar attached to the ratchet on top. Occasionally, you will find used basket presses in very good condition although very old. A very good buy

Bladder Press

Some home winemakers now use bladder presses once used only by commercial wineries.   Similar to a basket press except there is no ratchet mechanism to exert pressure. In the center of the stainless or wood basket is a rubber bladder that is inflated by either water or air. This expanding bladder exerts pressure on the grapes from the center. This bladder press can be very expensive.

Hydraulic Press

These presses again are similar to the plain basket press but uses hydraulic pumps to exert pressure.

Crusher

One of the important pieces of equipment for the advanced or more serious winemaker is the crusher-destemmer. The crusher-destemmer is used when fresh grapes are used. Many suppliers will crush and stem grapes that you purchase on-site for a fee. After you buy your grapes, they will crush and destem, leaving you with only the juice to take home. If you crush and destem your own, you can vary the skin contact time. This adds flavor and color. This is a matter of choice, do you only want the juice from the fresh grapes or do you want to control and vary all aspects of your winemaking. I prefer crushing and destemming myself. Still available are the hand-operated crushers that simply crush your grapes. I used a hand-operated crusher (that my grandfather motorized) for many years. These are much less expensive than the crush-destemmer, which does both, the stems dropping out of one side. With red wines, a crusher-stemmer is needed. While we want the berries crushed, the stems add the bitter tannin flavors are not wanted.

BOTTLE CORKER

Hand Held Corker

A small corker will be needed not matter how much wine you make. These small hand held corkers are suitable for bottling up to maybe 25-50 gallons. These hand operated corkers are very inexpensive (20 dollars) and available at you wine making supply shops. It is best if you soak the corks in hot water before corking with the hand held bottle corker.

Floor model Corker

Floor model corkers are great for the home winemaker making from 50-200 gallons of wine. The floor corker can be used to fill about 300 bottles an hour while the hand held model is very slow. Pre-soaking is not needed with the floor model corker.

Thermometer

Another nice tool is a floating thermometer to keep track of your grape must while fermentation is active. Very useful when trying to maintain a cool white wine fermentation.

> ➤ Another nice item is to use a self-stick LCD thermometer on your primary fermentation container. This makes it very easy to monitor fermentation temperature.

Bottle Sterilizer

A bottle sterilizer is a handy gadget that I won't do without. The one I use has a plastic reservoir that holds the sterilizing solution, either chlorine or sulfite. Inside the reservoir is a small plastic hand operated pump. You place the empty bottle on top of the pump and depress several times which shoots the cleaning solution into the bottle. This is much faster than using the funnel and pouring into each bottle.

Bottle Rinser

A bottle rinser is attached to your kitchen faucet. You place your empty wine bottle onto the rinser, which then shoots hot or cold water into the bottle, and since the bottle is inverted, the water drains at the same time. When you remove the bottle, the rinser shuts off automatically.

Bottle Draining Trees

You can make your own racks to drain your bottles after being sterilized and rinsed, but the bottle trees are made from easy to clean plastic and store the bottles at the correct angle so that they drain. There are several sizes available ranging from 40 to 90 bottle capacity. Again, its not needed but makes life much easier if your bottling a lot of wine.

Capsulers or Heat Tunnels

For that finishing touch to your new wine you will need a capsuler or heat tunnel. These items just heat the shrink capsules over the tops of your wine bottles. Similar in size to a hair dryer and hand held. This is truly a luxury item. An old heat plate can also shrink the capsules on your bottles but this is much faster.

Carboy Brushes

Carboy brushes are available to assist in cleaning the inside of your carboys They are long handled bottlebrushes that fit inside the carboy. They come in a variety of sizes.

ADVANCED VARIATIONS

The variations of winemaking techniques are limited only to your imagination. The one variation I think of very often was basically taught to me by my great grandfather, Pasquale DePasque. He was a very good winemaker, or at least made wine that everyone fully enjoyed and raved about.

I was in probably about 14 or so when I was asked to help great grandpa make wine. I was driven to his house, and we proceeded to pick the grape from the arbor in his yard. From the yard, we went to the cellar with bushels of freshly picked grapes. We both sat on little chairs in his poorly lite cantina, wine cellar, having poured us both small glasses, similar to juice glasses, of wine. His wine cellar had a built in masonary grape press that I vaguely remember.

Great grandpa was a methodical man, the year before having taught me how to make Christmas wreathes. Although I never learned, he would make all the Italian cheese from ricotta to mozzarella to the hard cheeses. Today, I wish I had.

Having been making wine with my grandfather for years, I was expecting that we had to use the grape crusher. To my surprise, bunch-by-bunch, we removed the berries from the stems. Hour after hour, berry by berry, keeping the berries intact. These berries were put in an open barrel to ferment. One of the things I remember most was that my hands were purple from all the grapes. The next day in school I was kidded very much about the purple tint.

After several years of making wine again, using my grand father's crusher, fermenting skins and all, I began to read about winemaking. At some point the fact that the stems contain a lot of tannins hit me and I remembered Great grandpa DePasque.

If you want to make a very fruit tasty soft wine, try our variation. I've changed it a bit, but it is very nice. Hand pick every berry from the stem. It's a lot of work and very time consuming but I think its well worth the extra effort. The resulting wine matures very early, is very soft and a pleasure to drink by Christmas. As you pick the berries off the stems, try not crushing them. As the grape are removed from the stems, put them into your primary fermentation container. I try to keep about 70% of the berries intact. You will need some of the berries crushed so that there is some juice in order to start fermentation.

I start fermentation by adding my started yeast 12-24 hours after adding sulfites and I let the fermentation continue. I gently punch the cap down twice a day. Try to keep the berries intact. I continue keeping the grapes on the skins for up to 21 days. You do not have to keep the grapes on the skins for 21 days, and can press soon as the sugar falls to 5 brix.

After the first few days I blanket the must with Carbon Dioxide or Nitrogen which is not absorbed, covering the entire fermentation tank in plastic to contain the carbon dioxide. Plastic can be taped over your tank using duct tape to seal the tank. Everyday I open the tank, and punch down the cap as I finish, again re-tape the plastic cover and blanket with carbon dioxide. At the end of 14 days, start tasting the wine daily before you punch down the cap. At some point, at anywhere between days 18-24, the wine will change. With this change, the wine softens. You will have a wine with deep intense color, soft in tannins and fruity. I have found Nitrogen to be better since it is not absorbed by the wine.

This method is a combination between carbonic maceration and extended maceration, both of which I'll explain. The first advanced variation is blending.

Whole berries during fermentation

SEPERATION OF FREE RUN and PRESSED JUICE

Another advanced technique is to keep your free run juice from the pressed juice. Once primary fermentation is complete and you remove the juice from your primary fermentation container, keep it separate. Allow this juice to complete fermentation by itself. Now, instead of mixing the juice that your are extracting by pressing with the free run juice, keep this separate also. Keep this pressed juice separate for secondary fermentation all the way through your final racking.

At this point, you can bottle these two wines separate. You will be amazed at the differences in taste. It's the same grape, same yeast, same temperature but it is like 2 totally different wines. I always enjoy letting friends taste two wines made in this fashion. They are always surprised at the differences.

If the free run wine is lacking a bit or needs extra body, start blending the 2 wines together.

BLENDING

Most home winemakers limit themselves to making only varietal wines. Most of the great wines of the world are blends of two or more varieties of grapes. A single variety can be greatly improved by blending with another.

Remember the most important rule in blending is the blend must be superior to each of the varietals separately. Take Alicante grape for example, not usually known as a great wine, but add a small percent to Cabernet or Merlot or an early season Zinfandel, its adds so much color.

Try adding Valdespena or Merlot to Cabernet. The lower tannins found in Valdespena or Merlot and its drinkable much sooner soften cabernet. Most commercial operations make their blends from wines that have been fermented separately. I make most, but not all, of my blends in the old European style of blending the grape during the crush. Many times, after your wine has aged a bit, before bottling in the springtime, you will notice your wine is lacking somewhat. We make several types of wine, so it's easy to add 10-15 percent of another wine to the lacking wine. When blending, take notes, use small quantities for your trials to see if you like the blend.

Try determining what blends you might like. Buy some single varietal wine, even though they only need to be 70% of any varietal to be labeled as such, and try your hand at blending. Try blending your home made wine of one variety with a commercial single variety. Then next year, make a new blend of what you discovered.

Try blending similar variety grapes from different locations such as a Zinfandel grown in Southern California with a later season Zinfandel from

Northern California. You can blend wine from different years as some wineries do to make a consistent tasting wine or champagne. The possibilities are endless. The following are some commercial and homemade blends to give you an idea.

Beaujolais

Beaujolais, French wine that is made from Gamay noir. This is a light, fruity wine. Beaujolais Nouveau is fermented by the carbonic maceration method. This wine is also made from Gamay noir.

Sauterne

Sauternes are sweet white wines from France. Sauterne is a blend of Semillon (70%) and sauvignon blanc (30%). This wine is made from the very ripest grape, infected with botryis. These wines can have up to 40% residual sugar.

Chianti

A red wine from Italy. Chianti is a blend of the red grapes, 80- 88% Sangiovese, up to 10% Canaiolo or Cabernet sauvignon, with a minimum of 2% of the white grapes Trebbiano and Malvasia.

Super Tuscans, such as Brunello

The red wines known as the super Tuscans. These wines are a blend of Sangiovese and up 10% Cabernet or Merlot. These wines are then aged a minimum of 36 months in small barrels.

Vin Santo

Vin Santo (holy wine) is from Tuscany, Italy. This dessert wine is made from the dried Trebbiano (50-75%) up to 5% Malavasia grape and up to 45% Pinot Blanc or Chardonnay or Sauvignon Blanc. This wine can range from very sweet to dry.

Southern Rhone, such as chateauneuf du pape

These full-bodied red wines come from southern France. These reds are a blend of mainly Grenache with Syrah added for longer life. This wine has a minimum of 12.5% alcohol without added sugar. This wine is usually fermented without destemming and some producers use carbonic maceration to ferment. The cap is pushed down frequently along with hot fermentation.

Bordeaux Wine

Destem grape.
Fermentation temperature of 86 F
Punch the cap a minimum of 3-4 times per day to extract maximum color.
Post fermentation maceration. Allow one week to sit on skins
Free run wine is stored
This pressed juice will be used and stored separately.

HOME MADE WINE BLENDS

Over the years, we have experimented with many types of grapes and blends. Some blends worked and tasted great, some did not. Some of these blends are traditional blends used by home winemakers. As with most home winemakers, the different grapes are fermented together.

Grandpa Joe De Franco's Barbera/Petit Sirah Blend

This time proven blend consists of 80% Barbera along with 20% Petite Sirah. It produces a very deep red wine with full taste. I personally like this blend very much.

Barbera/Merlot

Another great blend is made of 80% Barbera and 20% Merlot. A very smooth red blend.

Italian Red Blend

This blend is based on an Americanized version of Chianti. It's very good and will hold up to hearty meals. The blend consists of 25% Alicante, 25% Petit Sirah, 40% Carignane and 10% Muscat.

Cabernet /Merlot

This produces a Bordeaux style wine. This blend consists of 80% Cabernet and 20% Merlot.

Cabernet/ Valdespena

These blends soften the hard bite that is present with new Cabernets. The Blend consists of 80% Cabernet and 20% Valdespena

Merlot/Cabernet

This blends greatly improves some of the plain Merlot, which at times lacks color and adds some deep flavors. The blend consists of 80% Merlot and 20% Cabernet.

Ruby Cabernet/ Zinfandel

This hearty blend will satisfy those who enjoy intense deep red wines with lots of body. The blend consists of 50% Ruby Cabernet and 50% Zinfandel.

Italian Red Blend

Another Americanized blend from an Old Italian recipe consists of 70% Zinfandel, 20% Muscat and 10% Alicante. This is an excellent everyday wine.

Rich's Blend

Over the years, I developed this blend. As you can see, I like the Petit Sirah and use it in many of my blends. This blend produces a very rich, full-bodied wine that can age for many years. This blend is comprised of 33% Carignane, 33% Petite Sirah and 33% Zinfandel.

Rhone Valley Blend

From France's Rhone Valley, this blend consists of 37% Grenache, 25% Cabernet Sauvignon, 19 % Syrah, 19 % Alicante.

Rhone Ranger Type Blend

This famous red blend consists of 33% Petit Verdot, 33% Syrah and 33% Mourvedre (also known as Mataro)

French Style Bordeaux

This is the typical red blend from Bordeaux France. Consists of 75% Cabernet Sauvignon, 15% Merlot and 10% Cabernet Franc.

Merlot/Valdespena

This blend which consists of 70% Merlot and 20% Valdespena and 10% Alicante is a personal favorite. The wine is smooth yet very heart with lots of flavors. The Alicante adds color to a sometimes-disappointing color of Merlot.

White Luna Blend

From the famous blue bottles, this white blend consists of 50% Chardonnay and 50% Pinot Grigio.

CARBONIC MACERATION

Carbonic maceration is another variation in the making of wine. This process will produce a light red wine that is very fruity with low tannin and are ready to drink very soon.

To begin, crush and destem about 10% of the total amount of red grape you are planning to use. You will need a tank of carbon dioxide or nitrogen gas. These small tanks are available from most gas supply stores. The gas is very cheap and you pay a few dollars to rent the tank, plus a deposit for when you return the tank.

Once you crush and destem about 10% of your grape, put those in your fermentation container and add your yeast. Put the remainder of your grapes, uncrushed, whole into your fermentation container. The best is a stainless tank with adjustable lid or any type container you can make airtight but has an air lock installed so that excessive carbon dioxide is released. Seal up the container but you will need a way to blanket the inside with carbon dioxide. We use a small piece of pipe that we slip down along the adjustable lid.

The temperature of the tank must be 85 degrees and the simplest way is to wrap the tank with an electric blanket. Continue fermenting sealed and at 85 degrees for 3 weeks. This is the method used to make Beaujolais Nouveau. You're ready to press.

EXTENDED MACERATION

Extended maceration is simply allowing the grape skins to soak in the must for extended periods of time. In order to extend maceration with out the grape skin from rotting, you will need to protect the cap and must with carbon dioxide. Although carbon dioxide is a by-product of fermentation, it is not enough.

Just as with carbonic maceration, you will need to get a small tank of carbon dioxide or nitrogen gas from your welding gas supply shop. As I said, it's very inexpensive.

With extended maceration, you will be allowing the skins to soak in the juice for up to 22 to 24 days. Everyday punch the cap down twice a day and blanket with carbon dioxide or nitrogen. You will know when its time to press, as the wine will change taste. Once the wine changes taste, press within 12 hours. You will notice the change, the wine will suddenly soften to your taste. The finished wine will have great color, soft in taste and fruity. In addition, pressing will be very easy since the skins have softened and very little pulp remains on them.

Just as with carbonic maceration you will have to seal the top of your fermentation container. The container does not have to be sealed until fermentation has slowed. The best is a stainless tank with adjustable lid or any type container you can make airtight but has an air lock installed so that excessive carbon dioxide is released. Seal up the container but you will need a way to blanket the inside with carbon dioxide. We use a small piece of pipe that we slip down along the adjustable lid of the stainless tank.

Plastic can be taped over your tank using duct tape to seal the tank. Everyday I open the tank, and punch down the cap, as I finish, again re-tape the plastic cover and blanket with carbon dioxide.

This wine is fantastic, try it and you will make it every year as we do.

SUR LIE or AGING on the LEES

Sur Lie is French for aging on the lees. The lees referred to are yeast lees that settle out of the juice during processing. Some wines such as Chardonnay are fermented in the barrel to add complexity. When fermentation is complete, the yeastells die and settle to the bottom. With most wines, this is when we would begin racking to remove the wine from the lees. With Chardonnay for example, the winemaker would allow the wine to remain in the barrel on the lees, dead yeast cells, to acquire some additional flavors. The time period can be from a few weeks to 4-6 months of more.

COLD SOAKING

Nowadays you hear a lot about cold soaking. Cold soaking is a very simple process used originally in Burgundy, France. It is thought that you will extract more color and flavor through cold soaking.

To cold soak, crush and sulfite your grapes. The principle is to allow the crushed grapes to remain at 40 degrees for about 48 hours prior to fermentation. After the 48 hours, you will inoculate the must with yeast and then begin to raise the temperature. You then ferment at normal fermentation temperatures.

BARREL FERMENTATION

Barrel fermentation is a technique used primarily on white wines such as Chardonnay. The fresh pressed juice is placed in wood barrels and allowed to ferment. This works very well for white wines since there are no seeds or skins involved in the primary fermentation. Red wines can also be partially fermented in barrels. By pressing your must a bit sooner and allowing your red juice to finish fermenting in the wood barrel.

There are several reasons why you would want to ferment your wine in a wood barrel. The first reason is that your wine will be protected from oxygen. Another reason is that you can obtain a more controlled wood flavor from the oak barrels. The wood flavor will be softer than if you matured your wine in wood barrels. At the same time, this wine can be aged Sur lie (on the lees), which will limit the amount of wood tannins added.

CO-PIGMENTATION

For centuries, Italian winemakers have added small amounts of white grapes to their red blends to produce Chianti or their own similar blend. This technique was also used in Burgundy and Rhone.

You would think that by adding a small amount of white grape, you would dilute the red pigmentof the red grapes. Instead, the addition of the small amounts (1-%-2%) of white grapes would intensify the red color as in Chianti or Burgundy.

The whites used in Chianti are Trebbiano and Malavasia. In the Rhone hermitage reds, Rousanne and Marsanne are used and in Burgundy, Pinot Blanc or Pinot Gris is used.

This practice has almost been totally abandoned commercially but is still continued by the traditional home winemakers. Over years, many experts decided that the mixing of small amounts of white grapes with the red did not add to the finished wine.

This has now again changed. Recent research has shown that the color of weaker reds can be enhanced by the use of small amounts of white grapes. Co-pigmentation has been used for hundreds of years; it's an old technique, but try it. For many of the old timers, it was their "wine secret" on how much white was added. I've had many homemade Chianti's, all made in the old traditional methods that are unique and very good.

CLARIFYING ADDITIVES

The purpose of clarifying agents is to assist you clear wine that has not fallen bright and clear on its own. Red wines given enough time and racking will fall clear and usually brilliant clear. White wines are usually much more stubborn but given enough time to settle out, they too should clear. Only after given enough time to naturally fall bright and clear, should you try the various clarifying agents. Use them sparingly and I recommend try just a test batch before putting clarifying agents in your entire batch of wine.

They are several common clarifying agents that work very well. In France bull's blood was used to clarify red wine, but this practice was somewhat halted with the outbreaks of mad cow disease and others.

Bentonite Powder is basically a type of clay. Normally, bentonite is used after fermentation and you would add about 1 to 2 grams per gallon of wine. As with all wine chemicals, read the manufacturers label directions. The key to using bentonite to add this powder to water, and let it sit a few hours. It is very sticky and thick otherwise. After it is rehydrated, stir into your wine and rack again in a few weeks.

Isinglass powder and liquid are again, common clarifying agents. This agent is used primarily for white and sparkling wines. Again, read the label instructions. This is somewhat easier to use due to the fact; it takes under an hour to rehydrate.

There are many other fine-clarifying agents on the market, the are easy to use and follow the label directions. Most owners of winemaking supply shop are very knowable about their products.

COMMON CLARIFYING AGENTS AND EFFECTS ON WINE

Egg Albumen	Reduces astringency	½ egg white per 5 gallon
Gelatin, 100 bloom	Reduces astringency, removes tannins	.5-1.0 gram per gallon
Bentonite, powder	Clarifies and provides heat stability	1-2 grams per gallon
Casein, Potassium Caseinate	Clarifies and reduces color, reduces browning	Follow directions,
Tannin	Clarifies and reduces color	Add to white wine when using gelatin
Sparkolloid, powder	Removes hazes	0.5-1.5 grams per gallon

| Isinglass, powder | Used mainly in white wines | 0.015-0.07 gram per gallon |
| Polyclar VT | Removes some brown pigment | 1-3 grams per gallon |

FILTRATION

Do you need a filter? I believe the best wines are wines that fall bright naturally. Can an expert tell if a wine has been filtered? I don't think most experts could tell if they were given a glass of wine and you asked was this wine filtered. If you have a filtered wine and an unfiltered wine, both the same wine and you ask was this wine filtered, the expert would probably notice a difference in the same wine. From my own biased point of view, I think my wines change slightly if I have no other choice but to filter the wine. Red wines usually will fall bright and clear while whites wines are much more difficult. There is nothing wrong with a white wine with a slight haze if you are considering just the taste. We Americans expect our white wines to be perfectly brilliant and crystal clear and in fact many bought wines are not only brilliant clear but also lack flavor. I am biased and think homemade wines far surpass most commercial wines in overall quality. Whites wine can be difficult and stubborn to clarify, and in some cases a filter is best. Experiment, try a clarifying agent first, do a few test runs using the various clarifying agents. In some cases, the use of clarifying agents will also strip the wines of some flavors so use them sparingly. There are several filters available for the advanced home winemaker and can range in cost from $100 to several hundred dollars. You should remember that filtration is never used to make up for lack of proper winemaking techniques. Of course brilliant clear wine is what we strive for, but I accept and enjoy plain clear wine, free from any haze.

COLD STABILIZATION

One important step in wine making is *COLD STABILIZATION*. In areas that get cold, you don't have to do a thing as long as you allow your wine to age for 2-3 weeks at 30-40 degrees. If you live in warm areas, you can use an old refrigerator to cold stabilize your wine. Wine is usually cold stabilized after the first racking and before the second racking usually in the early spring.

Cold Stabilization simply precipitates the bitartrate from your wine. During cold stabilization the acidity is reduced slightly and more importantly, softens your wine. The tartaric acid found naturally in your wine, will precipitate out during this cold spell and settle to the bottom of your fermentation tank or carboy. This harmless crystalline precipitate is Potassium acid tartrate (KHT). You will find a hard settlement at the bottom of your carboy or fermentation container. These crystals are harmless, but give a poor appearance to your wine bottle.

After cold stabilization, the second racking is much easier. Instead of the soft, fluffy lees found during the first racking, the lees after cold stabilization will usually have the crystals that basically seal the lees at the bottom.

After each racking, I always about 40-50 PPM of sulfur dioxide or campden.

SUGAR ADDITION

If for any reason, you would like to or have to add sugar to raise the Brix of your wine must, be sure to use white cane sugar.

> If sugar is needed for white wine, it is added prior to fermentation. For red wines, the sugar is added just after pressing, since you only then know the volume produced.

Sugar addition also known as *Chaptalization*, **which is simply to increase the final alcohol content,** by the addition of sugar before and or during fermentation. In England, this practice is also known as *Amelioration* and in Germany, it is known as *Verbesserung*.

How much sugar to add? See the chart below to determine how much sugar should be added to every gallon of wine must in order to raise the Brix a certain amount.

For example, you want to raise the Brix of you grape must. You've taken a sample and measured the Brix. You found the Brix to be 20.5 and would like to raise it 3 Brix to 23.5 Brix. So, if you have 4 gallons of juice, multiple 4 times .25 pounds of sugar (amount needed to raise 3 Brix), which equals 1 pound of sugar needed.

Number of Brix to be raised	Amount of sugar to add
1 Brix	.084 pound per gallon
2 Brix	.17 pound per gallon
3 Brix	.25 pound per gallon
4 Brix	.336 pound per gallon
5 Brix	.42 pound per gallon
6 Brix	.50 pound per gallon
7 Brix	.60 pound per gallon
8 Brix	.67 pound per gallon

As a fast rule of thumb, one cup of sugar is equal to .456 pound of sugar.

MALO-LACTIC FERMENTATION

What is malolactic fermentation? Malolactic, ML, fermentation is a secondary fermentation that converts the naturally occurring stronger malic acid that is found in wine into weaker lactic acid and carbon dioxide. Adding a culture known as Leuconostoc or Lactobacillus available through wine supply dealers can induce Malolactic fermentation. Usually ML fermentation is desired in red wines and a few whites such as Chardonnay.

Many old winemakers including my Grandfather believed that certain wines or grapes would start to ferment again in the spring. Many vintners believed that the wine was waking up in the spring just as the grapevines did. Although they did not know that ML fermentation was occurring, they recognized "that's a good wine, it woke up". What was actually occurring is natural malolactic fermentation. Once a wood barrel has had ML fermentation, it will usually reoccur. Occasionally, ML fermentation will occur after the wine is bottled causing the wine to either push out the corks or show a slight sparkling when poured. If ML fermentation is going to occur naturally, it will occur in the spring with warming temperatures.

Why induce ML fermentation? ML fermentation does a few things to red wine. The Total Acidity of Wines that have gone through ML fermentation will usually be about 0.2 to 0.4% lower in total acidity. At the same time, pH will be raised about 0.2. This will give you a softer wine with added complexity. ML fermentation is a good way to lower the total acid and add complex flavors.

For ML fermentation to occur, you must obtain the culture and follow the manufactueres instructions. Some culture's must be added at the beginning of fermentation while others must be added towards the end of fermentation. Remember, for ML fermentation to occur, the temperature mustbe above 60 degrees F and the sulfur level must be below 20ppm. Additionally, the pH should be between 3.1 to 4.5. ML fermentation should be complete in about 10 days. Do not induce ML fermentation if potassium sorbate was used. This will produce an off odor in your wine.

SULFUR and pH

For the first time winemaker, 50 PPM of sulfur should suffice to kill unwanted yeast and act as an antioxidant without getting too technical. For the advanced winemaker you must realize that there is a relationship between pH and the amount of sulfur that is needed to perform the same function.

➢ As we know, the ideal pH for red wine is 3.5 and for white wines, the perfect pHis 3.2. Overall, the lower the pH, the less sulfur is needed and conversely, the higher the pH, the more sulfur needed to have the same sterilizing effect.

How much sulfur is too much? Some people with very sensitive noses can detect as little as 100 PPM. As long as you keep below that level, you should be OK. As with any chemical, use as little as possible to do the job. According to the FDA, wines can contain up to 350ppm. For the home winemaker, that is entirely too much. The FDA recommendation is for commercial wineries and very frankly, many homemade wines far surpass commercial wines in taste and quality. You will soon agree with that modest statement after you have made a few batches of your own homemade wines.

pH and Amount of Sulfur- Red Wines

pH of grape juice	SO2 needed Potassium Metabisulfite	Amount of campden / 1gallon
2.80	15 PPM	1/3 tablet
2.90-3.00	20-25 PPM	½ tab
3.10-3.20	30-40 PPM	2/3 tab
3.30-3.50	50 PPM	1 tablet
3.60-3.70	60-70 PPM	1 1/3 tab
3.8	100 PPM	2 tab

pH and Amount of Sulfur- White Wines

Ph of grape juice	SO2 needed Potassium Metabisulfite	Amount of campden / 1gallon
2.80	20 PPM	½ tablet
3.00	40 PPM	2/3 tablet
3.20	60 PPM	1 1/3 tablet
3.40	70 PPM	1 1/3 tablet
3.60	80 PPM	2 tablets
3.80	120 PPM	2 ½ tablets

Potassium Metabisulfite	1.4 grams ¼ teaspoon	6.2 grams 1 teaspoon

LABELS

Now again is time for family involvement. Labels are the finishing touch for your homemade wines. When I started bottling my wine, my labels were very simple in design. Over the years, along with teaching my two retired friends, George Talarico and Rudy Riccardi on how to make wine, our wine designs became much more sophisticated thanks to George's daughter Lori, a graphic designer.

Just this year, our label won first prize in the commercial division at the American Wine Society Conference in Cleveland, Ohio. My wife's niece, Missy Boyer, who is an artist, did the artwork for this label. Have a young artist in the family, have him or her design a label or design a simple label yourself.

Besides being the finishing touch, labels are needed to keep track of what is in the bottle. Don't rely on your memory, it does not work, I tried. A simple label should have the year made or bottled, what type of grape and your name, if you want.

You can find computer programs to design labels or use a graphics program to design your label. It's so simple now. At one time, use used self-adhesive labels that just could not be removed. They were beautiful but not functional since I recycle my wine bottles. Try using glue that comes off easily in water. Many wine supply catalogs and shop also sell labels, blank labels, everything you need to properly label your wine.

➢ Use a 1 x 3 self-adhesive label upside down on the plastic capsule to identify your wine while still in the wine rack. Since the 1 x 3 label is around the neck of the bottle, you can easily find the wine you want from the rack.

CAPSULES

That last finishing touch to your new wine is the capsule. Capsules are very inexpensive and add that store bought-finished look to your wine. They are available in a wide range of colors and we usually color code our different wines with different color capsules. It's much easier to find different types of wine in the rack when color-coded.

The plastic capsules are heat shrinkable and available at all winemaking shops. In order to shrink the capsule, you can use an old hot plate. Just slip the capsules over the top of the bottle, lower the top of the bottle to the heat plate and it shrinks, fitting your bottle perfect. If you want a luxury item, they sell specific capsulers or heat tunnels just for capsuling your wine. Be Careful while heat shrinking. The red-hot heating elements will give a very nasty burn.

WOOD BARRELS

Should I use wood barrels. When I first started making wine on my own after my grandfather passed away, I used his barrels. That year, I ruined my wine, it spoiled. The following year, I bought a new "used" barrel and again had trouble with my wine. I then started using glass carboys and demijohns, and those unexplained troubles went away. As a youngster, I never really paid much attention to my grandfather when he prepared the barrels, although, I did help carry the empty barrels and wash them. He had a special hammer to tighten the steel rings around a barrel, taping all around to tighten the barrels every year. When the barrel was emptied, sulfur strips were burned inside the barrel to sanitize the inside of the barrel. Some years, as in Italy, he waxed the inside of his barrels when they were getting old or developed leaks.

I prefer glass or stainless steel to store and age wine in. Why, they are easier to maintain and cheaper in the long run. Barrels must be replaced every few years. Unknown bacteria will hide in your empty wood barrels. Wood barrels cannot be left empty, as molds will grow. Leaks will develop and wine must be added to the barrel during aging, a process known as **topping off**. Topping off is simply adding wine to barrel that has been lost to evaporation. This is known as *ouillage* in France. Topping is usually done from to once every one to six weeks depending on barrel condition. Dropping stones in the barrel to replace the evaporated wine did this topping off of evaporated wine from the barrel in Germany. Lastly, many old time immigrants poured olive oil into their barrels to protect the wine from oxidation from air. This method was not very effective or helpful to the wine or barrel.

When looking at a barrel, the flat ends are called the heads. The body of the barrel, each individual slat or plank is a stave. The stave that has the bunghole is the bung stave. The metal bands that hold a barrel together are the hoops, with the hoop closest to the end called a head hoop. Part way down the barrel is the quarter hoop and the band closest the bunghole is the Bilge hoop.

What is the purpose of wood aging? Oak barrels will impart a roasted oak or aged vanilla flavor to your wine. Generally, red wines are better with a slight oak taste than white wines. Try using oak chips or powder. Be careful, as once oak is added, it will take years for that flavor to mellow out. Chips and dust will add the same flavor without the problems associated with barrels. The oak chips and dust will not leak or have mold.

The oak chips or dust are added directly to the wine. Usually dust is added during fermentation while oak chips are added during the aging period.

When you buy chips or powder, as with everything, follow the manufacturers instructions. With any oak, I would start with half the recommended amount. After a few weeks or months taste the wine, you can add more if you desire. Be careful with the oak, once it's added you can't get rid of the flavor, so, please, go slow with the oak.

I prefer the chips as the flavor is added much slower and you can make variations by toasting the oak chips or shavings in your oven. With both the dust and chips, you will add from 1 to 5 grams per liter, which is 4 to 19 grams per gallon.

➢ Just as a rough estimate, a teaspoon of oak dust will weigh about 1.2 grams while a tablespoon of oak dust will weigh about 3.6 grams.

Another option that works very well are oak sticks. The toasted sticks are about one foot long and are about one inch by one inch. The sticks are placed directly into your wine, but must be sanitized with a sulfur solution prior to putting into your wine. These should be allowed to soak in your wine for several weeks, be sure to check your wine occasionally for the amount of oak flavor.

➢ When using any of these oak products, I find it better to only oak a portion of your wine. Instead of oaking a full 5 gallons, oak a half gallon and slowly blend the oaked wine into the 5 gallons.

Oak for white wines

Very little or no oak	Moderate Oak	Maximum Oak
Riesling	Sauvignon Blanc, Chennin Blanc	Chardonnay

RECORD KEEPING

Another aspect for making constantly good wines is record keeping. I've been keeping records of my wine from the first batch I made. Knowing the date you bought the grape, gives you an idea when the grape might arrive the following year or even the location the grapes came from, with the grapes from southern California arriving sooner usually.

I keep track of all the variables in winemaking including the brix, acid, pH and a daily record of the brixreading and temperature. In this fashion, you can keep track of what is going on, any corrections you might have made and have a record of it. From year to year, you will build a nice record book of all the wines you made and can add comments years later on how the wine might have progressed, if you did not drink it all.

FERMENTATION RECORD

TYPE GRAPE_____DATE GRAPE RECEIVED_____

QUANTITY_____PRICE_____

CRUSHING

BRIX _____TEMPERATURE _____

TOTAL ACID_____ pH_____

SO2 ADDED_____AMOUNT_____

FERMENTATION

DATE and TIME YEAST ADDED____TYPE YEAST_____

DATE	TEMPERATURE	BRIX

Remarks:

_____

_____

DATE PRESSED _____ _____**days on skin** _____

AFTER FERMENTATION RECORD

DAYS FERMENTED _____

PERECENT ALCOHOL _____BRIX _____

RESIDUAL SUGAR _____ DATE_____

DATE	SO 2 ADDED	RACKING	TEMP

FINING or CLARIFYING AGENTS ADDED _____

ALCOHOL _____RESIDUAL SUGAR_____

REMARKS:

_____

_____

BOTTLES PRODUCED _____DATE_____

BLENDING NOTES _____

TASTING NOTES _____

PORT WINE

William III first discovered Port wines as a result of the excessive taxation on French wines being imported into England in 1693. In order to insure that Portuguese wines arrived in England in satisfactory condition, the wine merchants added a measure of brandy to each barrel to stabilize the wines.

It is said that in 1678, an Englishman, found a monastery in Lamego, Portugal, in which the abbot was adding brandy to the wine during fermentation, leaving some of the natural sugars unfermented. This produced the sweet, red port we know today.

Oporto, Portugal is the home of the full-bodied, sweet, fortified red wines called PORT. Port can legally only be made in Oporto, Portugal. Port is a sweet, fortified red wine. All over the world, port is enjoyed and made commercially. Law as to the ingredients and methods restricts commercial wineries in many places. The amateur wine maker can make this premium wine at home. Port can be stored for as much as 20 and 30 years.

There are several methods that a home wine maker can use to make a port style wine at home. The key to PORT is the natural sweetness found in grapes.

In order to produce port, rapid extraction of the color and tannin is very important. Fermentation time is very short, only 2 or 3 days. Because of this, fermentation must be vigorous in order to extract as much color as possible in this short time. The sweetness is the result of arrested fermentation. The fermentation is halted when the sugar concentration is still 9 to 12%.

Fermentation is stopped with the addition of alcohol, which kills the active wine yeast and preserving the natural sweetness of the partially unfermented grape juice. The final port should have a 17-20% alcohol level

To make a PORT style wine, you start fermentation of the must, juice and skin. Start by crushing and de-stemming your grape. It is very important to measure the specific gravity (Brix) in the beginning. As with red wine, the cap is pressed down a minimum of twice a day.

➢ Maximum color extraction will occur if the temperature is between 70 to 90 F.

When about half the sugar is fermented, now is the time to stop fermentation. Separate the juice from the must and press the must to insure maximum extraction. Adding 190 proof grain alcohol (available in most liquor stores stops fermentation). Add about 15 ounces of alcohol to each gallon of pressed juice. For lesser quantities, add about 120 ml of alcohol to each liter of juice.

At this time, put your port mixture in a clean carboy with an airlock on top.

After 24 hours, re-check your port mixture. Be sure fermentation has stopped (no bubbles in air lock). If the mixture is still fermenting, add another 1 % alcohol. Be sure to add 50 PPM of potassium sulfite after you check for fermentation.

Age and rack off sediment (lees).

One of the keys in making a Port style wine is blending. Several types of red grapes should be used, each fermented separately. Each aged and racked of separately. I usually make several types of red wine and pull about a gallon of each type for use in port. As I check the Brix (specific gravity) of my wine during fermentation daily. I take some juice and cap (floating skins) when the sugar is half fermented. I press the skins and add the alcohol. The balance of the must continues to ferment to dryness. During the aging process of your ports add oak chips to one of the bases.

After you have accumulated several base types of port, now is the time to blend. The best way is to buy a bottle of port, sit down, start tasting the purchased port and start blending your own. If you like, you can add about 2-4% brandy as you blend your different ports. This brandy adds a unique taste to you homemade port. 2% brandy is about 2 1/2 ounces per gallon. Slowly add the oaked base as you blend. Blend in small quantities and write down what you have blended. I usually make several combinations and after a week or so, I re taste my different combinations. At this time, I blend all the port.

Now is the time to bottle and age. Port can be aged up to 30 years (but mine never ages for more than a year or so. It's very good. Now, if you don't use pure alcohol and need to use brandy or another distilled spirit, you will have to determine how much spirits to add.

FORTIFYING WINES WITH ALCOHOL

If you are planning to make fortified wines, you will have to understand the math of **Pearson's Square**. Pearson Square will give you the amount of alcohol or spirits that you must add to raise the alcohol level in order to fortify a wine.

The best way to fortify a wine is with pure alcohol if you can get it. The purpose of fortifying wine is to raise the alcohol level without adding flavor. Wines such as port, vermouth and sherry need to be fortified.

		8
A 40		**D** **(C-B)**
	C 20	
B 80		20 **E** **(A-C)**

To use Pearson Square, replace each letter in the box above with the number that corresponds below.

A = the alcohol content of the distilled liquor or alcohol that you will use to fortify the wine. This could be 80 proof brandy or 40% alcohol.

B = the alcohol content of your wine that you will be fortifying. This could be the alcohol content of your wine, say 12%

C = is the intended alcohol content of your wine after fortifying. This would be your intended alcohol content of your finished fortified wine, say 20%

D = C minus B. In this case, 20 (c)—12 (b) which would equal 8

E = A minus C. In this case, 40 (a)—20 (c) which equals 20.

The letter D equals the amount of Brandy or other alcohol spirit that you need to use. In this case, you need 8 parts (D) of alcohol.

The letter E equals the amount of your wine that you will be using. In this case, you will need 20 parts of your wine.

A single part maybe a cup, quart, liter or gallon. 8/20 (D / E) would equal 2/5. So, with this equation, you will need 2 quarts or liters of brandy added to 5 quarts or liters of wine to make a total of 7 quarts or liters of fortified wine.

AQUADDE WINE, PIQUETTE, SUGAR or SECOND WINE

Another type of wine that has been around since the Romans is AQUADDE or PIQUETTE wine. This wine is also known as second wine or sugar wine. This is a second wine made after you had already pressed the grapes. The grapes still contain some flavor and color, particularly if you did not press the grapes very hard. This wine is to be consumed as soon as clear and is a way to make a bit more wine at minimal cost. The second wine is very drinkable while young, but do not mix this with your first wine, keep it separate.

Once your initial batch of grapes is pressed, removed the pomace from your press and put them back in the primary fermentation container. The grapes that have been pressed are called **POMACE**. Now add about the same amount of water as the juice you had already pressed from the grape. Stir the water and grape pomace together. Now add enough sugar to raise mixture to about 21 BRIX. Now, retest the second wine for TOTAL ACIDS, and add acid blend to bring the acid level up to the proper level between 0.6% to 0.85%. For red wines, start with 0.65% acid and with white wines; start with 0.70% acid. Wine with less than 0.6% acid taste flat to most people and wines with over 0.9% have too much acid for enjoyable consumption

Occasionally, my grandfather would make this wine, more just for the challenge I think. It actually turned out pretty good. The major problem was that it tasted very good, but once you started drinking your regular wine, the second wine could not compare. In addition, if I remember, back with my grandfather, there was no acid testing and lemon juice was added by taste to correct the acid level in the wine.

Years ago, when I first started making wine by myself, I would always make AQUADDE or second wine. A good friend of the family, who at the time, I considered very knowledgeable about wine consumption, enjoyed my aquadde, second wine very much, the wine being less intense and lighter than my other wines. I was very happy to bring them many gallons of my aquadde.

Sweeten your wine

At some point, you will find that the wine you made is just too harsh, dry or astringent. One of the ways to cut the dryness is to sweeten your wine. Most people cannot determine sugar / sweetness at under 1%, but the sweetness will give the impression of a mellower wine. Perhaps you want to make a sweet dessert wine.

The best way to sweeten your wine is to use sugar. Mix 2 cups of sugar into 1 cup of water, stirring until fully dissolved. I would make a few samples to try different amounts of sugar water added to your wine. Be sure to mark each sample with the amount of sugar water added. Add the sugar water in different amounts to each of your small samples. You can taste each of the 4 samples, but wait till the following day to determine which you prefer.

After you determine the sweetness level that you prefer, and are not making a sweet wine, but just mellowing out your wine, add the proper amount to the remaining wine. At this point, you will need to add **Potassium Sorbate**. This is a yeast inhibitor for wines with residual sugar. Potassium sorbate is usually used at the rate of 1-1/4 teaspoon per gallon, but always using according to label direction. Be sure to also add Potassium Metabisulfite at this time.

> ➤ To help soften your wine, try sweetening you wine. I'm not talking about making a sweet wine, but just a very small amount to soften your wine. Some award winning wines have small amounts of residual sugar that does finish the wine nicely.

Specific Gravity for various wine sweetness'

Dryness	Specific Gravity at bottling
Very dry	0.992—0.994
Dry	0.994—0.996
Medium dry	0.996—0.998
Medium	0.998—1.002
Sweet	1.002—1.006
Very sweet	1.006—1.030
Not fully fermented-stuck	1.030 and over

NO CHEMICAL STABILIZING FOR SWEETENED WINES
PASTEURIZATION

For those who would like to use chemical additives at the minimum, there is a way to stabilize your wine after sweetening. Without stabilizing your wine in some fashion, your wine will begin fermenting again sugar is added.

Pasteurization will kill off the live yeast cells and stop your wine from starting fermentation. Pasteurization is a very simple practice that can be done by the home winemaker. Once your wine is sweetened and bottled, you can cork the wine as usual. Now without potassium sorbate, this residual or added sugar will begin fermentation. Once you have you wine corked, fill a canning or stockpot full of water. You will need a candy or frying thermometer that can be attached to the pot immersed in the water. You can place a few bottles in pot once the water temperature reaches 150 degrees. The bottles of wine must be kept at 150 degrees for 20 minutes. Try to keep the bottles pretty much covered with water. After 20 minutes, place the bottles on their sides to allow the cork to be pasteurized. Allow the bottles to cool slowly and your wine has been pasteurized.

TESTING FOR RESIDUAL SUGAR

Your hydrometer is not effective to check your wine or adjust your wine for residual sugar. The easiest way is to get a CLINITEST KIT that is used by diabetics. These kits can be obtained from your winemaking supplier along with directions and the color codes needed to interpret the results and are simple to use. These kits are effective up to 10% residual sugar.

Vin Des Fimes

EXTRA COLOR FOR YOUR WINE

Sometimes for one reason or another, your red wine is lacking that deep color. In France, a mixture called a teinturier or tinting wine is used to deepen the color. If you can, obtain fresh or dried elderberries.

Take the fresh elderberries and put in a cooking crock with a few inches of water and cover. Put this covered dish in a warm, 200-degree oven for 1 hour then remove and allow to cool. For dried elderberries, allow to rehydrate and proceed.

The next morning, again, put the cooking dish back in the 200-degree oven for another hour. This can be repeated until the juice is extracted fully. After extracted, strain the liquid off.

Now, add enough sugar to bring this mix to 30 brix and ferment. This "wine" is meant only to tint your wine, very little is needed.

If you don't want to go through the trouble of making your own color enhancer, there are products made from grape skin extract and elderberry. There is a product made from grape skins and does not add tannin that is called exberry and is in liquid form.

FRUIT WINES

This book is primarily about grape wine. Recently I heard a minister talk about the Last Supper and the miracle of turning water into wine and how winemakers get to watch that miracle every time wine is made from grapes. Making wine from grapes is a miracle of sorts. No other fruit naturally turns to wine as does grapes. When you make wine from other fruits, basically you must follow a basic recipe like making bread. With any one of the ingredients missing, neither bread nor wine will be made.

With all wines, always start with good, sound ripe fruit.

Probably, the easiest non-grape wine to make is from apple cider. Fresh, non-pasteurized cider, although the government in its never-ending knowledge is starting to require that apple cider from the mill be pasteurized.

Fresh apple cider will usually have a sugar content of 8-11 brix This is actually too low for a wine, so sugar must be added. Remember the section on chaptalizing or adding sugar. You will want your apple wine to finish up with about 12-12 ½ percent alcohol, so you will need to add enough sugar to bring the cider up to 20-22 Brix This would be true with all fruit wines. As a rule of thumb, one cup of sugar is equal to .45 pound of sugar

As with all fruit wines, be sure to check the acidity with your acid test kit, follow the manufacturers directions. The proper range should be 0.7—0.8 % acidity. Usually, apple cider will be a bit low in acid, so you might have to raise it. As a rule of thumb, one ounce of malic or tartaric acid will raise the acidity of 5 gallons of juice about 0.1%.

If you are making 5 gallons of apple wine, start with 6 gallons of good cider. After checking the brix, adding your sugar, testing and adjusting the acid. Now, be sure to add 1 campden tablet per 1 gallon of juice. Wait 24 hours before adding your yeast. Be sure to add pectic enzyme (1 tablet). I usually use champagne yeast and it works quite well. Ferment till dry, checking hydrometer until reading 1.000 or less.

Put into primary fermentation container, cover. I use a 7-gallon carboy with air locks.

Wait 2-3 weeks after fermentation stops and rack off gross lees
Add Sulfur Dioxide 20-30 PPM
Cold stabilize
Rack again in spring
Bottle and drink

When I think of fruit wine, I think of my days as a youngster. My grandfather would go to the fruit market during the early summer when peaches where there ripest. The juicy peaches were peeled and sliced. These slice⸱ peaches were put in a bowl covered in red wine and allowed to soak for a fe⸱ hours. At dinnertime these refrigerated peaches, soaked in red wine were served The peaches were a beautiful red and served in dessert glasses along with th⸱ wine. After eating the peaches, the flavored wine was sipped. Try it; it's a grea⸱ summer time treat. This tradition of fresh fruit in wine was brought from Italy b⸱ my grandfather that still continues in our family until today.

Vin Santo, Italian Dessert Wine

A very fine dessert wine that we make is similar to the Italian Wine called Vin Santo. A sweet, very hard Biscotti cookie is served as dessert with Vin Santo wine. The biscotti are then dunked into the wine and enjoyed. My winemaking friend George R. Talarico and I make this high alcohol recipe yearly. It makes a great gift and is best to sip with a few homemade biscotti.

George Talarico's Vin Santo

15 pounds	Raisins, chopped
8 pounds	Sugar, white cane
14 Teaspoon Vinacid O	
2 Teaspoon Yeast Nutrient	
2 Teaspoon Pectic Enzyme	
4 Teaspoon Tannin	
6 Quarts Warm Water	
8 Campden Tablets	Crushed
9 Quarts Cold Water	
1 Package Yeast	Red Star Premier Cuvee (Up to 18% alcohol)

To begin, chop the raisins, this is a tough sticky job, but needs to be done in order to get the full flavor. Place the chopped raisins in your primary fermentation container, for this a 6-gallon plastic pail works great.

Add the hot water and Vinacid O, add the sugar and still until completely mixed.

Add the remaining ingredients except for the yeast. Prepare the package of yeast in 1 cup warm, not hot water. Allow the yeast to dissolve in the water, adding 1 teaspoon of sugar. In about ½ hour, you will see the yeast foaming, now its time to add to your mixture.

Cover your primary fermentation container loosely with clean plastic and keep at room temperature.

Press down the cap of floating raisins twice a day. Check the brix with your hydrometer every two days.

Once the Specific Gravity reaches 1.020, its time to remove the raisins. If you do not have a small fruit press, get a straining bag, available at beer making shops. You can use the straining bag to squeeze the raisins fairly dry.

Now, rack the juice into a clean carboy. Remember to install your fermentation lock on top.

Check the Specific Gravity daily until it reaches 1.000. Now, since we know, wine yeast starts to die off when the alcohol level reaches 12%-14%, we need to fool the yeast so we can make a higher alcohol wine naturally.

First make sugar syrup, which is no more than 2 cups of sugar mixed into 1 cup of hot water, stirred until completely dissolved and cooled.

Whenever the specific gravity goes down to 1.000, add enough sugar syrup, so the specific gravity is raised to 1.010. You will need about 1 pound of sugar to raise the specific gravity about 0.010 in 5 gallons of juice.

Continue the sugar syrup feeding at least 4 times. You should finish this wine slightly sweet with about 2% residual sugar, but go according to your own taste.

Continue racking until clear, used bentonite to help finish clear.

Once the wine is clear, your ready to bottle in 375 ml bottles.

Joann's Hazelnut Biscotti for dunking in Vin Santo Wine

4 cups all purpose flour
2 cups sugar
2 teaspoons baking powder
6 eggs
4 tablespoons hazelnut liquor (Frangelico)
3 teaspoon almond extract
3-teaspoon vanilla extract
2 cups roasted hazelnut, chopped coarse, substitute almonds or walnuts if you
    prefer

Pre-heat oven to 350 degrees
Mix dry ingredients except nuts
Separately, mix liquid ingredients
Mix both wet and dry, until dough is stiff
Shape the dough into 2 logs about 14 inches long and about 2-3 inches wide
Place on greased cookie sheet
Bake for 20 minutes at 350 degrees

Remove from oven, allow to cool a few minutes, with a sharp knife, cut diagonal crosswise strips about 1 inch thick.

Place each strip back on cookie sheet, cook additional 15 minutes until golden brown.

Cool and store in airtight container.

ICE WINE or EISWEIN (dessert wine)

Icewine or Eiswein as it is called in Germany is a late harvest wine made from grapes pressed while frozen. German Eiswein dates back to 1794 in Franconia, Germany. Both Canada and Germany are known for their Icewine or TBA Eiswein. Usually Icewine is made from Vidal or Reisling grapes, but the home winemaker can also use muscat or Seyval. The regulations from various countries concerning their wines and processes, do not apply to the home winemaker.

To make Icewine, the grapes are left on the vine until after the first frost hits. These grapes are harvested after being frozen in the vineyard and then, while still frozen, they are pressed. German law states that Eiswein can only be made from grapes with a sugar content of 28 Brix in the unfrozen state. In Canada, the law states the grapes must be 32 degrees Brix in the unfrozen state. They are picked early in the morning while the weather is still fridgit. During both picking and pressing the temperature cannot exceed -8 degrees C. At this temperature (-8 degrees C) the individual berries will freeze solid as marbles. The grape is pressed while still frozen. The water in the berries is frozen solid. The thick concentrated juice is released during pressing that may take several days. This leaves a highly concentrated juice, very high in acids, aromatics, sugars and usually a wonderful deep gold color. This wine juice may start out with a sugar content as high as 45—50 degrees Brix. Commonly, Canadian Ice wine is started at 38-50 brix. Fermentation is very, very slow and can take months. Because of the high sugars and cold temperatures fermentation is difficult to start. Fermentation is stopped at 6%-12% alcohol with 20 percent sugar remaining.

> In Germany, some eisweins are as low as 6% alcohol while in Canada, 10% alcohol is about average.

Since most home winemakers do not have grapes growing, we are forced to buy wine grapes when we can. We can still make a wine very similar to icewine at home, at any time. There are company's that sell juice, just for making icewine, or you can buy wine grapes in season, and put them in your chest freezer as we do. It's not a true icewine, but it's as close as the home winemaker can get. Icewine is usually bottled in 375-ml bottles and can be very expensive to buy. This wine can be aged for 20-30 years.

In Ontario and in Germany, icewine is defined as naturally frozen on the vine. This means that in both Canada and in Germany, no other method of making icewine commercially is allowed other than the natural method. Commercially, no artificial freezing method constitutes icewine by definition or label.

The basic guidelines for making icewine are as follows:

The finished wine must, should have a Brix of 35 degrees or higher.
There should be residual sugar of 20 percent.
The alcohol should be derived only from the natural sugars from the grape.

➢ Under German wine law, Eiswein must start out at between 30 to 36 brix (depending upon growing area).
➢ The alcohol content should not be lower than 5.5%

FREEZER ICE WINE

Another method that works very well but is not true ice wine or Eiswein but tastes very good is our freezer ice wine. This method is called freeze fractionating. You can use grapes, but apples and pears also make a fine ice-wine. This little trick that works great is not new. For over 100 years, hard cider makers would allow their hard cider to freeze just the water in the cider. In this fashion, they were able to at least double the alcohol concentration in their hard cider. DO not do this, as the Federal Government will consider you a bootlegger. Concentrating the alcohol either by freezing or the old boiler still down behind the barn is bootlegging. We are not freezing the hard cider or in our case the wine but the raw, unfermented grape juice. The purpose of freezing the juice is to concentrate the sugars and flavors as nature does if you allow the grapes to slightly dry out on the vine. Since I don't grow grapes, not enough to make all the wine I need, other methods are needed.

The first thing you have to remember is that your concentrating the sugar, acid and flavor by freeze fractionating. If the brix of your juice is 10, you will be left with roughly 25% of your starting volume in order to achieve 40 brix

Now, if you're like most home winemakers, your hydrometer does not go up to 40 brix. The solution is very easy, simply dilute your juice sample with exactly the same about of water (2 ounces juice, 2 ounces of water) and use your hydrometer. After getting your reading, double the brix and that will be an accurate reading.

In the fall, when grapes are available, we crush and press our Riesling or Muscat grape. After crushing, we will add the sulfite. As with white wine, check the brix and acid and allow the grapes to settle over night, allowing the particles to settle and rack off the next day.

Now with white wine, you would add the yeast, instead, put the liquid juice into clean 5 or 6-gallon pails. These pails will go into your chest freezer. My wife loves this since it forces me to clean out the freezer, get rid of those trout you caught 3 years ago and those funny frozen chickens that were on sale a few years ago. Never fill the pails since you're going freeze the contents and must allow room for expansion. Once your juice is frozen, forget about it until the cold weather arrives or unless if you have an extra refrigerator.

The water in your juice will freeze and the harder it freezes the more water that will be frozen. Now comes the time to slowly defrost or extract the concentrated sugar. The best is if you can defrost this frozen juice while at 32 degrees. If you are trying to achieve 40 Brix, 32 degrees is perfect. You can go higher but your finished brix will be lower. The best way to defrost this juice (at 32 degrees) is to drill holes in the lid of your plastic bucket. I save my drilled lids from one year to the next, and just replace the solid lid that was used to freeze the juice. While maintaining the 32 degrees, keep your frozen pail upside down so that the frozen juice can slowly run out of the lid into another clean empty pail. As the juice melts, the first juice that is extracted will be very high brix, as the juice continues to melt, the brix will be lower and lower. It may take a day or even two for the dripping juice to get as low as 15 brix At 15 brix, stop melting the juice, refreeze and repeat this operation. Repeat this two or the times until you get to at least 35 or 40 brix. Now you can ferment this concentrated juice using good yeast. Try to keep a cool fermentation temperature of about 55-60 degrees.

Save the leftover frozen juice. This still contains some sugar and flavor and can be made into a mild wine if sugar is added.

As I mentioned before, apples make an excellent ice-wine. Cider is plentiful and readily available. Use the same process to make an apple ice-wine. It's very good. A point to remember, most cider is only about 5 or 6 brix, so take in consideration the amount of cider needed. It will take roughly 8 gallons of apple cider to wind up with 1 gallon of ice wine.

PROPER REHYDRATION OF YEAST

Most active wine yeast is packed in sealed 5-gram envelopes; similar to dried bread yeast. Each envelope is sufficient yeast for 5 gallons of must or juice. Do **NOT** pour the yeast directly into your grape must or juice.

To insure proper rehydration, pour the dried yeast into a cup of warm, about 105 degrees F, NOT HOT water. Wait about 30-60 minutes, and then stir. You will see the yeast starting to foam. You can now pour the rehydrated yeast into your must or juice. This is called **inoculation**. Since the yeast is a living organism, the yeast will multiply in your wine must, converting sugar into alcohol. Remember; wine yeast dies off at about 104 degrees.

Add your yeast about 24 hours after crushing and sulfiting your must. Red wine will stay in the primary fermentation container for 3-5 days for color extraction. White wines will stay on the skins for 24 hours and then be pressed.

If you are making more than 5 gallons, you can use the same 5-gram packe and grow your own yeast. One of the important aspects of making good wine i insuring that fermentation starts quickly.

> When yeast has plenty of air and the temperature is between 65 and 8 degrees yeast cells double every two hours.

We insure a good oxygen supply by punching the cap twice a day on re wines. Below 60 degrees, yeast reproduce very slowly. Temperatures over 9 degrees again slow yeast production and stops totally at 105 degrees. When th temperatures reach 140 degrees, yeast cells die off.

Soon as you finish the crush, take out about a gallon of must and allow t warm, placing it in a tub of hot water or along side the hot water heater.

After the one packet of yeast is properly hydrated in a cup of warm water now is the time, we will begin growing additional yeast cells. While the yeast i rehydrating get a gallon or so of your grape juice must that is warming. Add jus a small amount of SO2 Allow the must to warm to 100 degrees (place next to hot water heater or in warm water bath). After about 30 minutes or so, the yeas should be bubbling

Add 1 cup of grape juice to the rehydrated yeast, cover with plastic and allow to sit about an hour.

After an hour, mix the remainder of grape must into the growing yeast. By morning, you will have a healthy culture of yeast ready to add to your grape must.

WINEMAKING MISTAKES

The following are some of the more common mistakes that are made during winemaking. Hopefully, you will not encounter any of these problems, but read over them, to learn the mistakes.

1. Poor Sanitation

Probably the biggest mistake in winemaking is poor sanitation. Sanitize everything. As we discussed you can use metabisulphite or common house bleach. The purpose of sanitizing everything is to remove or reduce bacteria that will harm your wine. There are other sanitizers available at your winemaking supply shop. Follow the manufacturers instructions.

2. Unsuitable Equipment

Another problem many home winemakers run into is using the wrong equipment. Don't use old ceramic crocks to ferment or store your wine. Food Grade plastic is relatively inexpensive, buy it and use it only for wine. Clean your equipment before and after you use it. Stay away from old barrels that a friend's father used and have been sitting down the cellar. Don't use wooden spoons to mix your wine, they cannot be cleaned well enough.

3. Dirty Equipment

Clean all your equipment thoroughly before and after use. Everything must be clean. Don't clean it next week, put everything away clean. Sanitizing does not replace cleaning. In food processing plants, everything is cleaned, then sanitized just prior to use. Air-dry your equipment so mold does not grow. Remember that most of your equipment will only be used once a year, mold grows quickly in damp areas such as wine cellar or basement.

4. Yeast Addition

Another major problem is when to add yeast and how to reconstitute yeast. Do not add your yeast directly to your must. As we discussed, let your yeast grow in warm water then add to your wine must. Choose the right type of yeastfor the wine you are making.

107

5. Sulfite Addition

Adding too much or not enough sulfite is again, another major problem. Follow the manufacturers label instructions. Usually, the yeast is added about 24 hours after the must has been treated with sulfite. There are test kits available to determine the amount of sulfur in your wine. If you have added too much sulfur, get a pail, and start racking your must to remove some of the sulfur. Sulfur dissipates quickly in the open air.

6. Temperature Control

Starting to ferment your wine must at too high of a temperature will kill the yeast cells before the sugar has converted to alcohol. If the temperature is too low, your wine will not ferment.

Just as temperatures over 100 degrees will start to kill the yeast cells, temperatures below 50 degrees will also give you trouble. At these low temperatures yeast will grow very slow.

7. Not Adding Sulfite

Remember to add SO2 every time you rack your wine. This will help in the prevention of stray bacteria found in the air. Again, follow the recommended levels to add.

8. Keep Your Wine Containers Filled.

Another major problem is not keeping your carboys or barrels filled. Remember that air is needed during fermentation but after fermentation, air is the enemy to wine. Keep carboys filled to about 1 inch of the cork. Keep your barrels filled and check for leakage.

Carbon dioxide can be used to blanket your wine from oxygen. CO2 is heavier than air and is used by commercial wineries.

9. Hazy Wine

You will notice that some red and particularly whites wines, although racked very well, will always contain a slight haze. If the wine is not clear after the 3rd or 4th racking, trying using a clarifying agent.

10. Effervescence or Frissante Wine

Occasionally, you might see a slight fizziness in your bottle wine. Bottling your wine without complete fermentation causes this. Wine must be bottled after fermenting totally dry or follow the steps in sweetening your wine in order to stop fermentation.

11. Brownish Wine or Nutty Taste

Brownish colored wine or a wine with a nutty taste can be from oxidation. Possible causes are partially filled barrels or carboys, careless racking (allowing too much air) or low sulfite levels. (See 21 oxidized wine)

12. Sour Taste or Vinegar Smell

Acetic Acid, better known as vinegar. This again is caused by air. Air is the enemy to wine after fermentation. How is vinegar made? It's basically alcohol that's been given the opportunity to receive plenty of oxygen. Although fruit flies do carry the bacteria in vinegar, it's insufficient to turn wine to vinegar. Good thing for wine makers, vinegar does not start easily.

13. Burning Match Smell

When opening a bottle of wine and you suddenly smell sulfur, such as a burnt match, it could mean that there is excessive sulfur dioxide in the wine. Although sulfur dioxide is needed to prevent oxidation, you can't have so much that the wine has a sulfur smell. Swirling your glass of wine or re-racking the carboy full can lessen this smell. Most people can start smelling sulfur dioxide at 50 PPM.

14. Rotten Egg Odor

If you smell rotten eggs as you open your wine, this is HYDROGEN SULFIDE. This is a by-product of fermentation and usually caused by low nitrogen nutrient levels in wine or by excessive sulfur on the grape skins at crush time. If this is noticed soon enough during fermentation, add DAP, yeast nutrient and rack the wine. Keep racking, without adding the DAP, this should stop the problem. This problem if not cured at this point will continue will produce MERCAPTANS.

15. Natural Gas or Skunk Smell.

If your wine smells like natural gas, propane, skunk or even garlic, this is caused by Mercaptans. Mercaptans are formed from Hydrogen Sulfite. This is a major problem. Usually copper sulfate is needed to maybe remove this smell.

A simply way to add copper sulfate is to run your wine over a copper bowl or pot. This should add some copper sulfate.

16. Wet Cork or Wet Dog Smell.

If your bottled wine has a musty wet dog or wet cardboard smell that is called **CORKED**. This is caused by chlorine interacting with the cork. Never sanitize your corks with chlorine, but this usually happens during the cork manufacturing process.

17. Smells Like Nail Polish Remover.

If your wine smells like nail polish remover this is caused by Ethyl acetate. Combining ethyl alcohol with acetic acid forms ethyl acetate. AS the wine oxidizes, the first step is acetaldehyde. At higher levels, wine seems flabby. As the wine oxidizes even more, acetic acid will be formed and finally converting to Ethyl Acetate. There is no cure.

18. Smells Like Geranium.

If your wine smells like geranium leaves, this is caused by a chemical reaction. This flaw usually occurs in wines that have had potassium sorbate added to prevent refermentation in sweet wines. If the sulfite levels are too low and malolactic bacteria is present, this geranium smell will result. There is no cure.

19. STUCK FERMENTATION

This occurs during fermentation. If not corrected you will have a sweet wine that will produce effervescence or fizziness in your wine. Fermentation sometimes stops, usually from lack of yeast nutrient, but sometimes from being too cold. If you see no fermentation for 24 or 36 hours, and the wine still has sugar, first check the temperature. The temperature should be 65-70 degrees. This should start fermentation, if not, rehydrate an additional package of yeast. Add ½ teaspoon yeast nutrient (D.A.P.) per 5 gallons of wine must. This should re-start fermentation.

20 Finished wine with low acid

If your finished wine tastes a bit flat or flabby, it can be from low acid. I would add Citric Acid to the finished wine. Citric acid should not be added prior to fermentation. Citricacid is mild and is much better to add after fermentation.

21. Oxidized wine:

Oxidized wine is usually caused by carelessness on your part. In some manner you left the carboy or tank open to the air. The cork could have been dried out or loose or not keeping the SO2 content in the wine up to the required level.

If you bought just juice, the juice could have been oxidized to start with and was unnoticed.

For whatever the reason the oxidase can be reduced or eliminated, by the use of powdered skim milk. The procedure to reduce the oxidase is as follows:

A.

Determine the amount of wine to be treated. For each liter of wine measure out 0.5 GM of powdered skim milk into five- (5) ml of cold water. Mix well making sure all the skim milk is dissolved. IMPORTANT: It is important that you use POWDERED SKIM MILK, not whole milk.

B.

Bring the SO2 level of the wine up to the proper level.

C.

Stir the wine and while swirling the wine, add the skim milk solution.

D.

Continue to vigorously stir the wine. Make sure all the skim milk is well blended. Do not just pour the skim milk mixture on the surface of the wine, be sure to incorporate the skim milk mixture below the surface of the wine.

As soon as the skim milk is fully blended, you will notice brown curds in the wine.

E.

Put the fermentation or airlock back on your carboy. Let the wine to settle for about 1 week. Now is the time to prepare a bentonite mixture to clarify your wine.

F.

Rack the cleared wine into a clean carboy. Stir in your bentonite mixture Again, allow the wine to settle and rack again.

SERVING WINE

It's true that most wine is supposed to be served at room temperature. This does not mean today's home temperature of 70-72 degrees, but what was considered room temperature 100 years ago. 100 years ago, room temperature was 60-65 degrees. It is better to serve your wine on the cool side rather than on the warm side. Wine can always be warmed slightly with your hand holding the bowl of the glass. The ideal temperature to cellar and store your wine is 50-58 degrees. The term for bringing wine to room temperature is chambrer-ing.

Wine service temperature

41 - 50 Degrees	50—60 Degrees	65—70 Degrees
Rose, White Champagne Naturally sweet Sparkling	Light Red	Full bodied Red

DECANTING

Very often with homemade wine or well-aged wine, a sediment can occur in the bottle. This is a natural occurrence with unfiltered wine. There are basically two reasons for decanting wine.

The first reason is to separate the clear red wine from sediment, which has developed over time. Older wine should be drank and enjoyed shortly after decanting. If the wine is not decanted, the wine can be muddy or cloudy.

The second reason to decant wine is to permit a hard, young red wine to breathe to soften the mouth feel some. These young red wines will improve from decanting and allowing to breathe for a few hours.

Before decanting wine, bring the bottle to the table about 1 hour prior to drinking it. Keep the bottle horizontal and put it on the table were you will be opening it. Do not allow the bottle to roll off the table, place napkins on both sides to prevent the bottle from rolling.

Next, get you empty decanter, be sure it is clean and free from odors.

Now, 100 years ago, a candle was used to look into the bottle, but a flashlight or even an electric light will do. The purpose is so you can see the settlement inside the bottle as you decant. The candle is a nice touch if you have company, adding charm to the entire affair. So, at this point, light your candle or flashlight or light bulb and place it besides the bottle.

Now remember, your trying to move this bottle as little as possible, and as my grandfather used to tell me, "no shake". With the bottle still on its side, gently sink the corkscrew into the cork and screw it in.

Very gently, begin removing the cork, when the cork is almost free, lean the neck of the bottle up slightly, but keep the bottom of the bottle on the table. Go nice and slow and easy. Remember to lift the bottleneck enough so the wine does not spill out.

Once the cork is completely out, gently lift the bottle, remember my grandfather, "no shake", begin pouring the wine into the clean decanter, very slowly, having the wine trickle against the side of the decanter bottle, just as in racking wine, same principle. The candle or light should be under the bottle.

Once you see the first stream of cloudiness reaches the neck, stop pouring. You have decanted the wine and are ready to enjoy.

LIQUEURS

Although not part of winemaking, it was tradition in our family to make several different types of cordials or liqueurs. Several of the old recipes have been lost forever. My great grandmother would make Stregga, a cordial similar to Galliano at home. I've tried several times to make this, but this recipe has been lost from our family.

Many old timers made Grappa from the left over skins, seeds and stems, the Vinnacce or pommace. As in Italy, New Zealand and several other free countries it is still legal to distill your own alcohol. Distillation is illegal in the United States. This local art has thus evolved into many, very well made local specialty cordials.

Recently, my Aunt Josephine from Italy visited during wine season while we were making wine. It was very educational and enlightening hearing her explain how she still makes wine in Italy, the same way as my Grandfather did. During this visit, she brought some homemade **Limencello**. This is a lemon-flavored liqueur that is very good. Originally, she used grain alcohol, but now uses vodka. You can substitute the 100 proof vodka with ½ the amount of grain alcohol if you like. Once you try these liqueurs, they will become part of the extended family tradition.

With all of these homemade liquors or cordials, the longer they age, the better they are. I usually wind up trying them within a month or so after bottling, then allowing a few more months of bottle aging.

Over the years, I've had many homemade specialty liqueurs. A friend's grandfather would make a fig liqueur from figs in his yard. I've also had pear liqueur, which was excellent. All these liqueurs are basically made my macerating the fruit in alcohol and adding simple sugar syrup. Many of these cordials consisted of herbs and leaves from various plants to make liqueurs such as Stregga and Galliano.

Limencello
Lemon Liqueur

2—750-ml bottles of good quality vodka 100 proof
Or 1- 750ml bottle grain alcohol
16—large, sound good quality lemons using just the zest
5- cups water
4 ½- cups white sugar

Wash and clean the 16 lemons carefully. You will then peel the lemons, trying to peel just the skin. After peeling, remove **all** the white pith on the rear of the lemon peel. Cut the peels into 1-2 inch pieces.

Place the cleaned lemon zest or peels into a gallon glass jug. Be sure the glass jug is cleaned and sanitized. Add 1 bottle (750ml) of vodka. Cover and allow to sit in dark area for 30 days. Shake the mixture occasionally for better extraction, but not required.

After 30 days, make simple sugar syrup by boiling 5 cups of water; add the 4-½ cups of sugar once the water boils. Allow the sugar syrup to cool.

Now add the sugar syrup to the lemon peels in your gallon container. Add the second bottle of 100 proof vodka. Stir well. Again, close the gallon container and allow to sit in dark place for 30 more days.

After 30 days, strain the Limoncello through cheesecloth and discard the lemon peels. Bottle into screw cap bottles (cleaned vodka bottles) and you are ready to enjoy as an after dinner delight. This is very delightful. As my grandmother would say, "refreshing".

Another variation of Limoncello is **Rosolio**. This is very tasty and similar to Limoncello. The combination of ingredients sound unusual but is very good. The old timers made these unique cordials out of tradition and necessity. In many rural areas, these cordials were not available and if they were, they were very expensive. Every town made variations of many of these cordials.

Rosolio

2 ¼ cups of fresh whole milk
2 ¼ cups of grain alcohol
2 ¼ cups of Powered sugar
2 fresh sound lemons
½ vanilla bean

Wash and peel the lemons, be sure to clean away the white pith completely from both the rind and the lemon. Chop the lemons and remove the seeds

Chop the vanilla bean and mix into a glass container with the chopped lemons and rind and grain alcohol.

Add the powered sugar and then the milk. Stir and mix well. The milk will curdle but is expected.

Place in cool day place for 7 days, shaking the mixture every day. At the end of 7 days, strain the mixture through cheesecloth. After the first straining, you will strain this mixture through a paper coffee filter.

Now, bottle it and allow to bottle age for month or so. It's very good and unusual

NOCINO
Walnut Liqueur

This is a very traditional Italian liqueur that is made from fresh walnuts that are still in the outer green shell. These are immature fruit. Since these are not usually available unless you own a walnut tree, we will substitute shelled walnuts.

1—750ml Vodka 100 proof (use good vodka)
Or 375ml of grain alcohol

1- Pound of toasted walnuts (toasted in oven)
Whole walnuts will be quartered

1- Fresh cinnamon stick

1- Vanilla bean

4—Whole cloves

2—Cups of white sugar

2—Cups of water

Zest of 1 lemon, no white pith

Get a clean and sanitized jug about ½ gallon in size.
Lightly toast the walnuts in the oven for about 15 minutes and allow to cool.

Place all the ingredients except the sugar and water and vodka into the glass jug and allow to sit in dark place for about 2 months. Occasionally, shake the jar.

After two months prepare the simply sugar syrup and add to the Nocino.
Filter through cheesecloth and then a paper filter. Now you are ready to bottle and enjoy. Another variation is that you can substitute hazelnuts for the walnuts. I enjoy Nocino served cold after a great wild game meal.

These walnuts should not be thrown away. You can add some white wine and allow the wine to seep with the walnuts for a week or so to make that special nutty vermouth that is great for a martini. These nuts can also be roasted with chicken and are very good.

117

If you grow a lot of raspberries or can find some ripe raspberries, the following is very delicate and excellent after dinner cordial.

Lamponino
Raspberry Liqueur

1—750ml bottle Grain alcohol
2 ½ - cups white sugar
2 ¼ - cups water
1 ½ - pound ripe raspberries
Zest of 1 lemon

Cut the raspberries and place into clean glass jug. Make simple syrup by mixing the sugar and hot water. Add the lemon zest and alcohol. Mix all the ingredients together and place in cool place. Mix daily by shaking the jug. After 60 days, strain the mixture and bottle.

Again, these berries can be placed into some mild white wine. This gives a very nice flavor for a summer sipping wine.

Cigliegiolo
Cherry Liqueur

Another favorite that my grandfather made was Cherry Liqueur. In early summer, when the ripe cherries appeared it was time to make the liqueur. Although he had a cherry tree in his yard, I really believe the tree was used more as target practice, trying to keep the birds away with the old daisy air rifle.

1 ½ - pounds of sound ripe cherries
1—750ml good quality Vodka
2 ¼ - cups of white sugar
2 ¼ - cups water

As with all these recipes, start with simple sugar syrup, mixing the sugar into hot water and allowing to cool.

Place the cleaned cherries, whole, into a clean sterilized glass jug. Add the vodka and sugar syrup.

Allow to age. We usually save this treat until Christmas when the cherries are eaten first and the liqueur is enjoyed slowly.

Amaretto
Fast Almond Liqueur

This recipe was given to me by a friend, is very good and only takes 30 minutes to make. You can taste this next to the bought Amaretto and this is just as good.

Always start with good quality vodka if you are using vodka as the basis for any of your liqueurs.

This recipe will make one 750ml bottle of Amaretto.

½ - cup Brown sugar
1 - cup White sugar
1—cup Water
2 ½ - Tablespoons of almond extract
1—Tablespoon vanilla extract

Prepare the sugar syrup by boiling the water and stirring in the sugars. Allow to cool.

After cool, add the 2 cups of good quality vodka and extracts into the sugar syrup. Pour into a clean, sanitized screw cap bottle and your done. This recipe is fast and easy. Put it in the liquor cabinet and your done aging.

ADVANCED WINEMAKING CHEMICALS

This section is basically last because except for sulfur dioxide, SO2, wine chemicals should be used only when required and at a bare minimum. The bottom line is that a good, well-made wine from sound grapes does not need any additional chemicals. There is no cure all for bad wine, except dumping it. Adding chemicals to wine are like taxes, less is better.

Occasionally, your wine might need a little help to correct minor problems or assist with clarifying.

> **As with all chemicals, READ THE LABEL and FOLLOW the label directions. Always, use food grade products.**

Pectic Enzyme

Pectin is found in many fruits and helps them jell after cooking like in jelly. In winemaking this pectin causes haze. Pectic enzyme helps the wine settle and clear much easier. Used in white wines to help remove the haze. It is best to keep pectic enzyme liquid refrigerated to preserve its strength.

Bentonite Powder

Is a type of naturally occurring clay that is used to help clarifying wine. Be sure to rack first if you will be filtering. This must be soaked in water for at least 24 hours prior to use

Sparkolloid Powder

Good for most hazes and has little effect on wine flavor.

Isinglass Liquid or powder

Used mainly for white wines to help in settling and reducing haze. I prefer the liquid form. Isinglass is made from fish.

Gelatin Powder

Used as a clarifying agent. Helps soften red wines and removes tannins. This will remove some color from red wines. When used for white wines, grape tannin should be added.

Silica Gel

Helps to form more dense lees when used with bentonite or gelatin. Often, a loose fluffy lees is formed that is difficult to rack.

Potassium Sorbate

Also known as Stabilizer. This is used to inhibit yeast activity in sweetened or sweet wines. This is added after fermentation. It is usually added just as your are sweetening your wine and about to bottle. Be sure to use sulfur dioxide when using this.

Calcium Carbonate

This is used to reduce the acidity in wines and musts. Read the section on reducing acidity. Calcium Carbonated is precipitated chalk.

Potassium Bicarbonate

Also used to reduce the acidity in wines and must.

Tartaric Acid

Used mainly to raise the acid in musts from warm climate grapes that are low in acid.

Malic Acid

This acid along with tartaric acid is found naturally in grapes. Can be used for apple musts to increase acid.

Acid Blend

You will find this in many wine recipes. This is a commercial made blend of Tartaric Malic and Citric acids. This gives a wine, its bite and helps preserve the wine some.

Citric Acid Powder

Is much milder than tartaric acid and is used to raise the acidity of your wine AFTER fermentation. Citric acid is found in small amount naturally in grapes.

Diammonium Phosphate Powder

Also known as DAP and is a nitrogen source needed for wine yeast growth. Basically, it is fertilizer for your yeast. Can be used during stuck fermentation to aid yeast activity.

Natural Tannin Powder

Use the natural tannin derived from plants. It will also help with clarification. This is added mainly to white wines before fermentation that lack the tannins found in red wines. Also used in fruit wines.

GLYCERINE

Glycerine will add some body and a slight sweetness to your finished wine. This is also sold as wine conditioner or finisher.

WINE GRAPE VARITIES

In this section, I will explain some of the wine grape varieties. Although this is boring at this time, you will need to know about the various types of grapes. Each type grape produces a very specific type of wine. The characteristics of certain grapes are transferred to the wine. Many people that enjoy wine know that certain grapes produce a particular flavor and aroma that they either enjoy or don't enjoy. Many wine affectionatos can identify the type of grape that was used to produce a certain wine. Cabernet for example has a very specific aroma (or nose) and taste. To begin, the California wine grapes are Vitis Vinifera, the same as the European wine grapes. Vinifera berries are larger, sweeter and usually better tasting than the other species.

RED VINIFERA VARITIES

Alicante or Alicante bouchet

Known for its red juice. Great for blending to add great deep colors. The red color is very intense and dark but has little acid and light in body. Usually blended to other varieties to add color to port and table wines.

Barbera

Originally from Piedmont region of Italy. The grape has very high acid and distinct character. Makes a great full-bodied wine, and stands up to tomato sauce.

Cabernet Sauvignon

Excellent balance and color and rich in aroma. Originally from Bordeaux region. France. Improves greatly with age and can be among the best wines in the world. Will be hard when drank young.

Carignane

Used mainly for blending. Is heavy bodied and full of tannin with medium color and acid. Used for making bulk table wines.

123

Carnelian

University of Southern California developed this. Is a combination o Cabernet Sauvignon, Carignane and Grenache. Will produce an early to drink flavorful, zesty, red wine. Can be light or full-bodied depending on technique.

Grenache

Used as a rose wine in France and is among the best. Usually, not enough color to be used as red table wine but great to blend with other grapes as in chateauneuf-du-Pape. Is a fruity wine and can be blended with Alicante to produce a full-bodied red wine.

Merlot

A medium red table wine. A distinctive, aromatic, spicy varietal wine Merlot is also used in blending of Bordeaux, adding fruit and a velvet quality to a wine otherwise a bit bitter.

Mission

Was first variety planted in California by Spanish missionaries. Has weak color and is not used alone for red wines. This grape is used for making swee white wines.

Petit Sirah

Excellent for blending. Will produce a wine of good quality with distinctive flavors with deep red colors and full-bodied. Is dry and lots of tannin. Not to be confused with Shiraz or Sirah.

Pinot Noir

With proper techniques and conditions, can produce richest, most velvety wines in world. Originally grown in French Champagne region. Used in Burgundy wines and to produce Champagne, without skins. Excellent

Ruby red

Very similar to Alicante. Used in blending because of red juice.

Ruby Cabernet

Is a combination of Cabernet Sauvignon and Carignane. Makes a fine varietal wine that is dry, fruity with good acid.

Valdespena

Originally from Spain. Produces a wine very similar to Zinfandel. Wine is a fine quality, clean red table wine.

Zinfandel

Used for a multitude of wines ranging from a blush to deep intense, aged wine. Also used in California Blends. Can be aged from 3-9 years.

WHITE VINIFERA VARITIES

Chardonnay

Originally from Burgundy, France. Produces full bodied, dry excellent wine. Is Premium California wine, aged in Oak.

Chenin Blanc

Used for many "jug" type table wines. Will produce either sweet or dry table wines.

French Colombard

Good for blending because of high acid. Used in Champagne and Brandy production. Used for producing quality wines.

Gewurtztraminer

Similar to Riesling that it grows well in colder climates. Small berries with acid level drops as grape ripens. Makes a fine dry or sweet wine.

Grey Riesling

New early season varietal. Is used to produce mild wines.

Malaga

Produces light dry white wine. Late season grape.

Malavasia

This grape is grown in California and in the Mediterranean. Makes dessert wines and also as fine aperitif.

Muscat

Originally from Italy and used in Asti Spumante sparkling wine. One of the most popular white grapes for home winemakers. Can make a variety of wines from sweet dessert to dry wines.

Palomino

Originally from Spain. Is used for dry Sherries and blending into white table wines.

Sauvignon Blanc

Produces a fine dry white wine with distinctive character. Can also produce sweet wines.

Semillon

Excellent for sweet wines, fruity and flavors of melon and fig bouquet. Very often blended with Sauvignon Blanc.

Thompson Seedless

Used by home wine makers to produce light white wine. Can be used for blending with reds to produce rose or with other whites,

Viognier

Originally from France. Used in Condrrieu wine. One of few higher priced white wines, better drank young. Produces excellent, high color, fruity white wine.

FRENCH HYBRID VARITIES

RED

Baco Noir

Can age very well. No foxy flavors, and good color. Was also known as Baco Number 1

Chambourcin

Good quality, better than most hybrids. Deep red colored and aromatic. Late ripening. Was also known as Joannes-Seyve 26205

Chancellor

Known as Seibel in France. Makes good roses's and reds. Can make dark red that can be fruity with low acid. Was also known as Seibel 7053

DeChaunac

Also known as Seibel 9549. Dark red in color. Can be thin in body but overall good quality.

Marechal Foch

Fruity red wine with black berries. Ripens early. Origin Alsace. Also was known as Kuhlmann 188-2

Baco Noir

Makes deep, intense full-bodied red wine. Can be slightly astringent.

Villard Noir

Used to blend in France. Was also known as Seyve-Villard 18315

WHITE FRENCH HYBRID

Seyval Blanc

Also known as Seyve-Villard 5276 in France. Has clean taste. Can be aged in oak along with malolactic fermentation. Can be fruity and clean if made in stainless steel or glass. Produces a light yellow wine.

Traminette

Similar to Gewurtztraminer well balanced sugar, pH and acid. Developed by New York State Agricultural Experiment Station.

Vidal Blanc

Similar to Riesling. Grown in Canada. Used for sweet, late season, and ice wines. Does not age as well as Riesling. Produces a light yellow wine.

Vignoles

High acid with high sugar content. Good for late harvest and ice wine. Was also known as Ravat 51. A Chardonnay hybrid.

Aurora

Well balanced and good quality. Has fair body. Also known as Seibel 5279

AMERICAN HYBRIDS

Concord

Pronounced labrusca that can be tart but deep red. Has foxiness as known in labrusca grapes. Used in jelly.

Catawba

Produced a white wine if pressed immediately after crushing. Is usually tart with labrusca foxiness. If left on skins will produce a rose or as champagne. Usually found in Eastern United States.

Niagara

Very fruity Labrusca. Produces a white wine, lower in acid.

Delaware

Similar to Traminer. Makes a soft dry wine with musky overtones.

Richard Schumm

EUROPEAN WINES

Most European or foreign wine is labeled by Controlled Appellations of Origin. A controlled appellation of origin dictates were the grape is grown, type of grape used and how the wine is manufactured and is regulated by the government.

As an example, Champagne is a sparkling wine made only in Champagne France. No were else can legally make a sparkling wine labeled champagne. You will occasionally see NY Sparkling wine labeled as NY Champagne, but this wine cannot be exported.

The purpose of the appellation system is to identify wines is to protect the reputations of vineyards and wine makers in specific areas. The French started the appellation system of identifying wines in the 1930's. The French system is the basis for the current European Union wine legislation.

These appellation systems do not affect the home wine maker.

Our discussion on the various types of European wines is only to give the home wine maker, an idea of the grapes used, in order to make similar wines at home. To date, researchers have identified about 5,000 varieties of grapes.

Wine can be classed by several factors.

Color such as red, white or blush

Alcohol Content Table wine is a still wine (non-carbonated) with less than 14 % alcohol, with dessert wine (fortified such as Port orSherry) ranging from 14% to 24%

Origin such as California, Napa, Washington, Bordeaux, Tuscany, New York State or Long Island. The term estate wine usually means the wine was produced from grapes grown at the winery where it is then bottled.

Sweetness can range from dry (no sugar) to semi-sweet to sweet (over 10% residual sugar)

Variety (about 5,000 varieties of grape)

This books deals with still or table wines, which means without carbonation or effervesion, so we will not bother with another classification, which is **Effervesion or** sparkling wine such as Champagne and carbonated

Burgundy

Burgundy is made up of 100% varietal grapes. In this case, Red Burgundy is made from Pinot noir. These wines are usually high alcohol, about 13%. In

France, sugar is very often added since Burgundy, France is a cool area. In cool areas grape have a shorter growing season and thus produce less natural sugar.

The white burgundy is made from Chardonnay. In this case also, sugar can be added to raise the alcohol level to 13%.

Beaujolais

Beaujolais, French wine that is made from Gamay noir. This is a light, fruity wine. Beaujolais Nouveau is fermented by the carbonic maceration method. This wine is also made from Gamay noir.

Sauterne

Sauternes are sweet white wines from France. Sauterne is a blend of Semillon (70%) and sauvignon blanc (30%). This wine is made from the very ripest grape, infected with Botryis. These wines can have up to 40% residual sugar. **Botryis** also known as the noble rot. This is a fungus that attacks the grape cluster causing bunch rot. Some very fine wines are made from Botryis infected grapes. This fungus can caused nearly ripe grape to dehydrate partially, which intensifies the sweetness and flavors.

Asti

A sparkling wine from Italy. This sparkling wine is made from Moscato grapes, which are called Muscat Blanc in California.

Barolo

A heavy red wine from Northern Italy. Barolo is made from the Nebbiolo grape.

Chianti

A red wine from Italy. Chianti is a blend of the red grapes, 80- 88% Sangiovese, up to 10% Canaiolo or Cabernet sauvignon, with a minimum of 2% of the white grapes Trebbiano and Malvasia.

Super Tuscans, such as Brunello

The red wines known as the super Tuscans. These wines are a blend of Sangiovese and up 10% Cabernet or Merlot. These wines are then aged a minimum of 36 months in small barrels.

Vin Santo

Vin Santo (holy wine) is from Tuscany, Italy. This dessert wine is made from the dried Trebbiano (50-75%) up to 5% Malavasia grape and up to 45% Pinot Blanc or Chardonnay or Sauvignon Blanc. This wine can range from very sweet to dry.

Northern Rhone, such as Jaboulet and Chapoutier

This wine is from Southern France. The red grape used is 100% syrah (not petit syrah)
The white grape used in Condrrieu is Viognier.

Southern Rhone, such as chateauneuf du pape

These full-bodied red wines come from southern France. These reds are a blend of mainly Grenache with Syrah. Added for longevity. This wine has a minimum of 12.5% alcohol without added sugar. This wine is usually fermented without destemming and some producers use carbonic maceration to ferment. The cap is pushed down frequently along with hot fermentation.

Bordeaux Wine

Bordeaux is made from Cabernet Sauvignon and fermentation temperature is high with maximum color extraction.
Wine ages much slower while kept at lower temperatures, and conversely, wine ages faster at warmer temperatures. In addition, storage container size affects how wine ages. Again, larger the container, more slowly wine ages.

ALCOHOL EQUIVALENCY

Since most states now have very strict drinking and driving laws, we that enjoy wine with our meals must be very careful. Usually a 4-ounce glass of wine contains the same amount of alcohol as a 12-ounce bottle of beer or a shot of hard liquor.

	Serving size	Alcohol
Wine 4 ounce	4 ounce	14.5 ml
Beer 12 ounce	12 ounce	14.5 ml
Hard Liquor 1.25 ounce	1 1/4 ounce	15.0 ml

CHARTS and CONVERSIONS

MEASURES AND EQUIVALENTS

CHEMICAL	¼ Teaspoon	1 Teaspoon
Acid Blend	1.2 grams	5.1 grams
Ascorbic Acid	0.9gram	4.6 grams
Bentonite	0.8 gram	3.4 grams
Citric Acid	1.1 grams	4.9 grams
Di-ammonium phosphate	1.2 grams	4.9 grams
Fermaid yeast nutrient	1.0 gram	4.6 gram
Gelatin powder	0.8 gram	3.2 grams
Isinglass powder	0.5gram	2.4 grams
Malic Acid	1.1 grams	4.5 grams
Grape Tannin Powder	0.6 gram	2.8 grams
Potassium Metabisulfite	1.4 grams	6.2 grams
Potassium Sorbate	0.6 gram	2.5 grams
Pectic Enzyme	1.0 gram	4.0 grams
Tartaric Acid	1.3 grams	5.0 grams

CONVERSION FACTORS

1 milliliter (ml) of water	1 gram (g)
1 ounce (oz)	28.4 grams
1 fluid ounce	29.6 milliliter
1 gram	0.035 ounce
1 pound (LB)	454 grams
1 pound	16 ounces
1 kilogram (kg)	2.2 pounds
1 gallon (US)	3.8 liters
100 liters (L)	26.4 gallons

CHEMICALS and CONVERSIONS

ACID REDUCTION

Acid reducing chemical	¼ teaspoon	1 tablespoon
Calcium Carbonate	0.5 gram	6.7 grams
Potassium Bicarbonate	0.7 gram	10.6 grams

Acid reduction of finished wine

Use Potassium Bicarbonate. Mix 3.4 grams per gallon of must to reduce acidity by about 0.1%.

Acid reduction of musts

Use Calcium Carbonate also known as precipitated chalk. Mix 2.6 grams per gallon of must to lower the acidity of the must by about 0.1%.

With both Potassium carbonate and Calcium carbonate never try to lower the total acid by more than .3%. If you do so, you can reduce so much tartaric acid that your wine is flabby.

COMMON CLARIFYING AGENTS AND EFFECTS ON WINE

Egg Albumen	Reduces astringency	½ egg white per 5 gallon
Gelatin, 100 bloom	Reduces astringency, removes tannins	.5-1.0 gram per gallon
Bentonite, powder	Clarifies and provides heat stability	1-2 grams per gallon
Casein, Potassium Caseinate	Clarifies and reduces color, reduces browning	Follow directions,
Tannin	Clarifies and reduces color	Add to white wine when using gelatin
Sparkolloid, powder	Removes hazes	0.5-1.5 grams per gallon
Isinglass, powder	Used mainly in white wines	0.015-0.07 gram per gallon
Polyclar VT	Removes some brown pigment	1-3 grams per gallon

Amount of Potassium Metabisulfite to add

The following will give you an idea on how much Potassium Metabisulfite powder per gram.

Amount	1 gallon	5 Gallon	50 gallons
1 Gram	150 PPM	**30 PPM**	3 PPM

The following will give you an estimate for 1/4 teaspoon of Potassium Metabisulfite powder.

Amount	1 gallon	5 gallons
¼ teaspoon (1.5 grams)	225 PPM	45 PPM

Always read and follow the manufacturers instructions.

AMOUNT OF SUGAR TO ADD TO MUST

Number of Brix to be raised	Amount of sugar to add
1 Brix	.084 pound per gallon
2 Brix	.17 pound per gallon
3 Brix	.25 pound per gallon
4 Brix	.336 pound per gallon
5 Brix	.42 pound per gallon
6 Brix	.50 pound per gallon
7 Brix	.60 pound per gallon
8 Brix	.67 pound per gallon

➢ **As a fast rule of thumb, one cup of sugar is equal to .45 pound of sugar.**

BRIX / SPECIFIC GRAVITY / POTENTIAL ALCOHOL

BRIX	SPECIFIC GRAVITY	POTENTIAL ALCOHOL
10	1.0395	5.57
11	1.0434	6.33
12	1.0475	6.90
13	1.0515	7.48
14	1.0556	8.05
15	1.0594	8.63
16	1.0639	9.20
17	1.0680	9.78
18	1.0723	10.35
19	1.0769	10.93
20	1.0814	11.50
21	1.0859	12.08
22	1.0903	12.65
23	1.0949	13.23
24	1.0994	13.80
25	1.1041	14.38

HIGHER BRIX

BRIX	SPECIFIC GRAVITY	POTENTIAL ALCOHOL
26.5	1.110	15.00
27.5	1.115	16.4
28.5	1.120	16.9
29.5	1.125	17.6
30.5	1.130	18
32.0	1.135	18.9

TEMPERATURE CONVERSIONS

Centigrade into Fahrenheit: multiply by 9, divide by 5, add 32
Fahrenheit into Centigrade: Subtract 32, multiply by 5, and divide by 9

WINE MAKING SUPPLIERS

Country Wines
3333 Babcock Boulevard
Pittsburgh, PA 15237

Presque Isle Wine Cellars
www.piwine.com/
9440 West Main Road
North East, PA 16428

Prespero Equipment Corp.
123 Castleton Street
Pleasantville, NY 10570

Corrados Winemaking Center
www.corradosmarket.com
600 Getty Ave.
Clifton, NJ 07011

F.H. Steinbart Co.
234 SE 12 Th. Ave.
Portland, OR 97214

Wine Art Indianapolis
www.wineart.com
5890 North Keystone Avenue
Indianapolis, IN 46220

Spagnol's Wine Supplies
1325 Derwent Way
New Westminister, BC. Canada V3M5V9

Semplex of USA
4171 Lyndale Ave. N
Minneapolis, MN

E.C. Kraus
Box 7850
Independence, MO 64054

Richard Schumm

Brew King
L.D. Carson Co.
463 Portage Blvd.
Kent, OH 44240

Vineco International Products
www.vineco.on.ca
27 Scott Street West
St. Catharines, Ontario, Canada

Alternative Beverage
www.ebrew.com
114-0 Freeland Lane
Charlotte, NC 28217

Napa Fermentation Supplies
575 Third Street,
Napa, CA 94559
(707) 255-6372

FROZEN MUST

Brehm Vineyards
www.brehmvineyards.com
932 Evelyn Avenue
Albany, CA 94706
Email: PbrehmVin@aol.com

AIR SHIPPED FRESH GRAPES

A1 Wine Grapes
Lodi, CA
1-866-A1grapes
www.A1winegrapes.com

JUICES

Walker's Fruit Basket and Press House
2860 Route 39
Forestville, NY 14062

SOCIETIES

The American Wine Society
3006 Latta Road
Rochester, NY 14612

A great organization with about 30% home wines makers. They have a quarterly journal as well as many publications.

PERIODICALS

Wine East
620 N. Pine St.
Lancaster, PA 17603

Practical Winery and Vineyard
15 Grande Paseo
San Rafael, CA 94903

Wine Maker
www.winemakermag.com
Post Office Box 469118
Escondido, CA 92046-9538

Richard Schumm

BIBLIOGRAPHY

American Wine Society, The *Complete Handbook of Winemaking.* Ann Arbor: G.W. Kent Inc. 1993

Amerine, Maynard A., and Joslyn, M.A. *Table Wines, The Technology of Their Production in California.* Berkeley: University of California: 1951

Cruess, W.V. *The Principles and Practices of Wine Making.* New York: Avi: 1947

Jackish, P., *Modern Winemaking,* Cornell University Press, 1985

Johnson, Hugh and James Halliday, The *Vintner's Art: How Great Wines are Made.* New York: Simon and Schuster 1992

Margalit, Yair *Winery Technology & Operations* San Francisco: The Wine Appreciation Guild 1996

Peynand E., *Knowing and Makings Wine,* John Wiley and Sons Inc. 1984

Robinson, Jancis *The Oxford Companion to Wine* New York: Oxford University Press 1998

Robinson, Jancis *Guide to Wine Grapes* New York: Oxford University Press 1996

Wagner, Philip M. *Grapes into Wine* New York: Knopf, 1986

Wagner, Philip M. *American Wines and Wine-Making* New York: Knopf 1956

Ough C.S. *Winemaking Basics* New York, 1992

WEBSITES

American Wine Society
http://www.vicon.net/~aws/

University of California-Davis
http://wineserver.ucdavis.edu/

Lalvin Yeasts
www.lallemand.com/

Scott Laboratories
www.scottlab.com/

Wyeast Labs
www.wyeastlab.com/

AROMAS

VARIETY	AROMA
Cabernet Sauvignon	Berry, black pepper, bell pepper, olives
Merlot	Berry,black pepper, bell pepper, olives
Malbec	Berry,black pepper, bell pepper, olives
Cabernet Franc	Berry,black pepper, bell pepper, olives
Pinot noir	Berry, strawberry jam
Riesling	
Chenin blanc	
Gewurztraminer	
Chardonnay	Spicy, fruity, apple, peach
Sauvignon blanc	Floral, fruity, citrus, apple,
Zinfandel	Berry, black pepper, raisin

INDEX

Amaretto, 119
Amelioration, 65, 84
Aquadde, 9, 64, 96
Biscotti, 7, 101, 102
Bollitura, 8, 43
Brix, 14, 21, 22, 23, 24, 30, 36, 44, 48, 65, 66, 71, 84, 90, 91, 92, 93, 94, 96, 98, 99, 101, 103, 104, 105, 135, 136
Campden, 18, 33, 38, 84, 86, 99, 101
Cap, 8, 28, 30, 32, 35, 43, 44, 46, 71, 72, 75, 78, 79, 93, 94, 101, 106, 116, 119, 132
Carbon dioxide, 9, 15, 30, 43, 44, 48, 64, 71, 72, 78, 79, 85, 108
Carbonic maceration, 72, 74, 75, 78, 131, 132
carboy, 4, 14, 15, 16, 44, 49, 53, 58, 61, 63, 64, 70, 83, 93, 99, 102, 109, 111, 112
Carboy, 9, 16, 19, 26, 33, 46, 48, 49, 50, 53, 54, 58, 61, 63, 67, 70, 83, 88, 108, 109
Chapeau, 43
Chaptalization, 65, 84
Chlorine, 26, 69, 110
Cigliegiolo, 118
Citric, 24, 65, 110, 121, 133
Cold stabilization, 49, 50, 65, 83, 84
Crush, 5, 6, 8, 9, 14, 15, 18, 19, 22, 26, 28, 29, 30, 31, 35, 36, 37, 59, 60, 63, 64, 67, 68, 73, 78, 80, 104, 106, 109
Crusher-stemmer, 35, 68
Decanting, 113
Demi-john, 4, 9
Drapeau, 31
Eiswein, 103, 104
Fermentation lock, 15, 26, 102

Foulage, 36
Free run juice, 8, 32, 35, 44, 46, 48, 60, 73
Frissante, 9, 108
Grappa, 9, 42, 115
Gross lees, 49, 50, 99
Hydrometer, 14, 22, 23, 33, 44, 98, 99, 101, 104
I Tres Pescadori, 54
Ice wine, 103, 104, 105, 128
Inoculation, 40, 59, 61, 63, 105
Lamponino, 118
Lees, 80, 84, 94, 121
Limencello, 115
Maceration, 43, 72, 75, 78
Malic, 24, 65, 85, 99, 121, 133
Malo-lactic fermentation, 85
Marc, 9
Must, 9, 12, 13, 14, 15, 18, 19, 20, 22, 24, 25, 26, 28, 29, 30, 31, 32, 35, 36, 38, 40, 43, 44, 46, 53, 54, 57, 58, 60, 61, 64, 65, 66, 69, 71, 73, 78, 80, 84, 85, 88, 89, 93, 94, 95, 97, 99, 103, 104, 105, 106, 107, 108, 110, 120, 121, 132, 134, 135, 138
Nocino, 117
Ouillage, 88
Ph, 18, 24, 25, 36, 66, 67, 85, 86, 90, 91, 128
Pigiatura, 5, 8, 36, 37
Pigment, 29, 32, 80, 81, 83, 134
Piquette, 64, 96
Pommace, 46, 115
Port, 93, 94, 95, 123, 130
Potassium Metabisulfite, 18, 26, 33, 38, 39, 86, 97, 133, 134, 135
Potassium sorbate, 85, 97, 110, 121, 133
Punching down, 32, 44

Racking, 9, 16, 48, 49, 50, 51, 52, 61, 63, 64, 73, 80, 82, 83, 84, 92, 102, 108, 109, 114
Rosolio, 116
Saccharometer, 14
Saccharomyces, 40
So2, 18, 38, 48, 86, 91, 106, 108, 111, 120
Soutirage, 49
Sulfur dioxide, 18, 38, 46, 59, 63, 84, 99, 109, 120, 121
Sur lie, 80
Svinare, 49
Tannic, 24, 29, 35, 44
Taralle, 6, 7, 10
Tarrale, 6, 7, 11

Tartaric, 24, 25, 49, 65, 66, 83, 99, 121, 133, 134
Titration, 24
Topping off, 88
Torchio, 9, 47
Travasare, 9, 50
Verbesserung, 84
Vin Santo, 74, 101, 102, 132
Vinnace, 46
Yeast, 6, 9, 15, 23, 28, 30, 31, 32, 33, 38, 40, 41, 42, 43, 46, 48, 59, 61, 63, 64, 71, 73, 78, 80, 85, 91, 93, 97, 99, 101, 102, 104, 105, 106, 107, 108, 109, 110, 121, 122, 133, 142
Yields, 28

About The Author

Richard Schumm, author of *90 Years of Winemaking* has been an amateur wine maker for over twenty-five years, continuing the De Franco Family Tradition.

The author started making wine as a youngster assisting his grandfather and great-grandfather in the art of winemaking.

Over the years, his homemade wines have won numerous awards using the techniques explained in *90 Years of Winemaking*

Breinigsville, PA USA
20 September 2009
224385BV00001B/4/A